six characters in search of an author

by

luigi pirandello

Translated by
Martha Witt and
Mary Ann Frese Witt

With Introduction by
Mary Ann Frese Witt

Italica Press
New York
2013

Italica Press Renaissance and Modern Plays Series

Italica Press, Inc.
595 Main Street
New York, New York 10044

Library of Congress Cataloging-in-Publication Data
Pirandello, Luigi, 1867-1936, author.
[Sei personaggi in cerca d'autore. English]
Six Characters in Search of an Author / by Luigi Pirandello ; translated by Martha Witt and Mary Ann Frese Witt ; with introduction by Mary Ann Frese Witt.
pages cm
Includes bibliographical references.
Summary: "A new translation of Pirandello's absurdist metatheatrical play "Sei personaggi in cerca d'autore" (1921), along with translations of two related short stories, the play's preface, a novel fragment of the same name and related correspondence. Includes an introduction and select bibliography"-- Provided by publisher.
ISBN 978-1-59910-276-4 (hardcover : alk. paper) -- ISBN 978-1-59910-277-1 (pbk. : alk. paper) -- ISBN 978-1-59910-278-8 (e-book)
I. Witt, Martha, translator. II. Witt, Mary Ann Frese, translator. III. Title.
PQ4835.I7S413 2013
852'.912--dc23

2013029923

Cover art: Rehearsal stage inside the theater of Heidelberg.

For a Complete List of Titles in
Italian Literature
Visit our Web Site at
www.ItalicaPress.com

six characters
in search of
an author

About the Translators

Martha Witt is an Associate Professor of English and Creative Writing at William Paterson University. She is the author of the novel, *Broken As Things Are* (Holt, 2004/Picador, 2005). Her translations and short fiction have appeared in multiple anthologies and international literary journals.

Mary Ann Frese Witt is Professor Emerita of Italian, French, and Comparative Literature at North Carolina State University. Her books include *The Search for Modern Tragedy: Aesthetic Fascism in Italy and France* (Cornell University Press, 2001) and *Metatheater and Modernity: Baroque and Neobaroque* (Fairleigh Dickinson University Press, 2013). She has published numerous articles on Pirandello and modern theater. In collaboration with Martha King, she is the translator of Pirandello's novel *Her Husband* (Duke University Press, 2000). She has translated and published contemporary Italian short stories in collaboration with Martha Witt.

In memory of Martha King,
mentor and friend

Contents

Introduction

"All the theater of an epoch has come out of the belly of this play," wrote a French playwright and critic in 1957.[1] He was referring not only to Pirandello's *Six Characters in Search of an Author* but in particular to the extraordinary staging of Benjamin Crémieux's French translation of the play by the Russians George and Ludmilla Pitoëff in Paris in April 1923. It was indeed an event that changed the very conception of what theater could be, eventually making possible the creations of theatrical innovators such as Samuel Beckett, Eugène Ionesco and Jean Genet in France and Harold Pinter, Tom Stoppard and Edward Albee in Britain and the United States.

The Pitoëff's production was also a life-changing event for Luigi Pirandello. Born in 1867 in a town called Caos near Agrigento in Sicily, where his father owned sulfur mines, Pirandello studied linguistics and literature in Rome and in Bonn, Germany, eventually marrying the daughter of one of his father's colleagues and settling in Rome. When the sulfur mines failed in 1903 and the loss of fortune apparently precipitated the mental illness from which his wife suffered for the rest of her life, Pirandello was forced to earn a living. He taught at the Magistero, a teacher-preparation college, and began his literary career at the beginning of the twentieth century not as a playwright but as a poet, short-story writer and novelist. Pirandello's best-known novel is *Il fu Mattia Pascal* (*The Late Mattia Pascal,* 1904). His fifth novel, *Suo marito* (*Her Husband,* 1911), partially based on the career of the Sardinian writer Grazia Deledda, contains numerous reflections on his longstanding and growing interest in theater.

It was in 1910 that Pirandello began to re-write some of his short stories as plays. The first one to be published and staged — written both in Italian and in Sicilian dialect — was the one-act *Lumié di Sicilia* (*Sicilian Limes,* 1913). He continued to write primarily short stories but adapted more of them for the theater. His first major three-act play to be produced in Rome was *Cosí è (se vi pare)* (*Right you are [if you think so],* 1917), again based on a

1. Georges Neveux in *Arts* (January 16, 1957). Cited by Paul Renucci in *Luigi Pirandello: Théâtre complet* (Paris: Gallimard, 1977), 1359. My translation.

short story. This play contains themes that will become important in Pirandello's later work, such as the relativity of identity and perception, the impossibility of knowing both the self and the other, and the simultaneously tragic and comic emotions that arise from such situations. Also in 1917, the well-known Italian actor and head of a theater company, Ruggero Ruggeri, produced and acted in his *Il piacere dell'onestà (The Pleasure of Honesty).* In 1918, Pirandello wrote and Ruggeri staged *Il giuoco delle parti,* the play that the actors in *Six Characters in Search of an Author* are rehearsing when the characters arrive, translated by Robert Rietty as *The Rules of the Game.* The Italian title literally means "the game of roles" and is concerned with the games and roles we play in life as well as in theater. The main character Leone, betrayed by his wife Silia, chooses to live without emotion but as if playing a role, representing himself as an empty eggshell. With the brief scene being rehearsed in *Six Characters.* Pirandello ironically pokes fun at those who criticize him for being too intellectual and incomprehensible an author.

Pirandello was thus a relatively successful Italian playwright, although not much known outside of Rome, and certainly not internationally, by the time he wrote *Sei personaggi in cerca d'autore: Una commedia da fare* in 1921. The subtitle, difficult to translate exactly into English, indicates that the main subject of *Six Characters in Search of an Author* is not "a play in the making," as it is sometimes called, but "a play to be made," which is never made. The action, such as it is, is composed of failed attempts to shape into a play the material narrated and acted out by the characters. The Italian word *commedia* can mean either a comedy or a play of any genre. While certainly not a comedy in any conventional sense of the word, *Six Characters* contains a number of comic elements, mingled with the melodramatic and the tragic. Its most daring and innovative feature was the introduction of "characters" — neither ordinary people nor actors — in an entirely onstage setting.

The script's originality was appreciated by the successful director Dario Niccodemi, who first staged it in Rome in the Teatro Valle, opening on May 9, 1921 to a full house. The evening, however, ended with the spectators rioting in the street outside the theater, some defending the performance but most deriding it, calling for the author to be sent to the madhouse. According to reviews, the audience had listened attentively during the first part of the play but eventually grew restless and started catcalling. Fewer and fewer people attended the subsequent performances, and by May 13 the play was shut down. Niccodemi's company, however, kept *Six Characters* in repertoire until 1927, touring with it in South America and Spain. It was successfully staged in Milan in September 1921, in Turin in December, and then in several European countries between 1921 and 1925, including performances in English translation directed by Theodore Komisarjevsky in London in February 1922 and by Brock Pemberton in New York, on Broadway, in October of that year.[2] Pirandello was thus already internationally known by the time the Pitoëffs mounted the French translation of *Six Characters* in April of 1923, but it was that production that established the play as both a revolutionary theatrical event and a modernist classic, catapulting the author to fame. That production was followed by another, also by a great European director, Max Reinhardt, in Berlin in December 1924.

Since the introduction of the proscenium stage in Europe — probably the first permanent one was the Teatro Farnese in Parma, Italy, built in 1618 — theatrical action had traditionally been confined to the stage area, with an invisible "fourth wall" separating the audience from the actors. Pirandello's plays, including his 1921 script of *Six Characters,* had maintained this convention. Under Pitoëff's direction, on the other hand, a few of the actors descended staircases into the auditorium, breaking through the "wall." Most memorably, instead of having the six characters enter and exit the stage conventionally, from backstage, he had them descend on and ascend from the stage in an elevator, a technological novelty at the time that enhanced the impression that the characters came from another world, or another level of reality. Dressed in black, the characters wore white make-up, so heavy and stylized that it gave the impression they were wearing masks. A white backdrop and the innovative use of lighting enhanced the non-realistic aura of the performance. Drawing on Symbolism and anticipating Surrealism, Pitoëff brought out the originality of Pirandello's text, in opposition to the conventions of the "well-made play" and of naturalism that still dominated the mainstream Parisian stage at the time. A play about a play that is never made, *Six Characters* may

2. See Jennifer Lorch's informative book, *Pirandello: Six Characters in Search of an Author,* Plays in Production Series (Cambridge: Cambridge University Press, 2005), 31–53.

in fact be read as a statement on the impossibility of writing and staging nineteenth-century plays in the twentieth century.

Although he was initially not convinced by all of the Pitoëff innovations, Pirandello came to adopt many of them in his considerably revised edition of *Six Characters* published in 1925. Differences between the 1921 and 1925 editions include several changes to the text, which the director had altered in order to make it less literary and more theatrical, the suggestion in the stage directions that the characters wear masks — no doubt influenced by the mask-like makeup used by Pitoëff's actors — more emphasis on the difference between the characters and the actors, development of theater-in-theater, and further breaking down of the fourth wall. Instead of having the characters enter from backstage, as in his 1921 version, or by elevator as in Pitoëff's production, Pirandello now has the characters walk down the aisle, through the audience and up the stairs to the stage. The Stepdaughter also exits this way — down the stairs and up the aisle — while the remaining characters reappear on stage, bathed in a fantastic green light. The Director and certain actors occasionally step off the stage, into the auditorium. One of Pitoëff's approaches that Pirandello did not agree with was the use of lighting to make the characters appear somewhat like ghosts or spirits. He wanted to stress that they were instead actually characters: what he called "created realities."[3]

Pirandello had long maintained that the author of a play, not the director nor the actors, should remain the supreme authority on a text's production. In 1924, however, he became involved in starting up a theater company in Rome, and by 1925 he was director of the Teatro d'Arte, the art theater. With his increased theatrical experience, his position on the superiority of the author was modified to embrace a more collaborative relationship between author and those responsible for producing the play. The company staged several plays by other writers before presenting Pirandello's revised version of *Six Characters* in 1925, but that play became

3. For more complete information on these changes, see Lorch, 57–61 and 80–85; Guido Davico Bonino, in the introduction to his edition of both texts, Luigi Pirandello, *Sei personaggi in cerca d'autore* (Torino: Einaudi, 1993), vii–xxxii; and Alessandro d'Amico, editor of the most recent Italian edition of Pirandello's plays, in his introduction to *Sei personaggi in cerca d'autore* in Luigi Pirandello, *Maschere nude* (Milan: Mondadori, 2007), 2:643–44.

its signature work, both in Rome and on tour in Europe and in North and South America. Marta Abba, lead actress in most of Pirandello's plays, as well as the love of his life, and Lamberto Picasso were celebrated for their performances in the roles of the Stepdaughter and the Father.

A member of the Fascist Party from 1923 until his death,[4] Pirandello fervently hoped that Mussolini would provide state support for the Teatro d'Arte, but il Duce, despite his professed admiration for Pirandello, failed to do so and the company disbanded in 1928. In between the two versions of *Six Characters,* he wrote another major innovative play, *Enrico IV* (*Henry IV,* 1921) about a contemporary young nobleman who believes himself to be (and/or acts the role of) the medieval emperor Henry IV of Germany. In 1933, he declared that *Sei personaggi in cerca d'autore, Ciascuno a suo modo* (*Each in His Own Way*, 1929), and *Questa sera si recita a sogetto* (*Tonight We Improvise,* 1930, dedicated to Max Reinhardt) formed a "trilogy of theater in theater." Although there are no "characters" in the second two plays of the trilogy, all three take place on a stage and are concerned with failed attempts to write and stage a play. Other plays by Pirandello include the comedy *Liolà* (*Liolà,* 1928), the "myth" *Lazzaro* (*Lazarus,* 1929), the drama *Come tu mi vuoi* (*As You Desire Me,* 1930), the libretto for opera *La favola del figlio cambiato* (*The Tale of the Changeling,* 1932), and the unfinished "myth" *I giganti della montagna* (*The Giants of the Mountain)* published posthumously in 1937). Pirandello received the Nobel Prize for Literature in 1934 and died in 1936.

By the end of his life then, Pirandello was a world-renowned author, beloved in Italy for his novels and short stories as well as his plays and admired abroad almost entirely for his plays, especially *Six Characters in Search of an Author.* That remains his most widely read and most produced play, and it is to a large extent the Paris production in 1923 and Pirandello's revisions to the script in 1925 that are responsible for his subsequent reputation as an influential modernist in the European avant-garde. *Six Characters,* however, did not begin as avant-garde art, but rather in the musings of a

4. The nature and extent of Pirandello's fascism continues to be an object of controversy. In my view, Pirandello's admittedly peculiar view of fascism had an important impact on several of his dramatic works. See my *The Search for Modern Tragedy: Aesthetic Fascism in Italy and France* (Ithaca, NY: Cornell University Press, 2001), 89–134.

relatively unknown Sicilian living in Rome. The writings included in this volume display its genesis. An early story, "Quando ero matto" ("When I Was Mad," 1902), mentions an author besieged by his characters, and in a 1904 letter, Pirandello writes that his characters are crowding around him in his study. The idea of characters as living beings in dialogue with their author first appears as a major theme in his short story "Personaggi" ("Characters"), published in a literary journal in 1906. Pirandello did not include it in any of his collections of short stories, and it has not previously been translated into English. Here, for the first time, a character speaks as...a character! The story is narrated in the first person by an author-character who appears to be Pirandello himself. Annoyed by the characters demanding to "live" in his stories, presented to him by his maid "Fantasy," the author interviews and finally dismisses the character Leandro Scoto after the latter pronounces a long-winded discourse on Theosophy, a popular spiritualist movement at the time.

Leandro Scoto would not reappear in Pirandello's writing, but the interaction between characters demanding to "live" in writing and an author who rejects them would be developed in his 1911 story "The Tragedy of a Character." In this story, the main character-character, "Dr. Fileno" (a more aggressive type than Leandro Scoto), gives a speech comparing the "birth" of characters to the birth of human beings, arguing that characters, who unlike humans may live eternally, are more "true," if less "real" than their flesh-and-blood counterparts. This speech, with a few modifications, will find its way into the mouth of the Father in *Six Characters* as well as into the 1925 preface to the play. In Pirandello's birth metaphor, the imagination *(fantasia)* of an author is the womb in which "seeds of life" will insert themselves and from which characters will eventually be "born."

A 1915 story, "Colloqui con i personaggi" ("Dialogues with Characters") also portrays an author who interviews characters and contains reflections on transitory life versus eternal art, but it has little direct relation to *Six Characters* and is not included here. Around this time Pirandello conceived the idea of writing a novel about an author who rejects the characters who come to him begging to be put into a novel. In a July 1917 letter to his son Stefano (then a prisoner of war), he gives the novel a title: *Sei personaggi in cerca d'autore: Romanzo da fare (Six Characters in*

Search of an Author: A Novel to Be Made). An undated fragment portrays the Father's thoughts and actions as he prepares to visit Madame Pace's brothel. This scene will not be included in the play but sheds light on Pirandello's conception of the character and the situation. The few lines in the letter to Stefano concerning the "novel to be made" make it clear that the six characters who come to the theater in Pirandello's play searching for an author are the same as those who were rejected by their author — no doubt Pirandello himself — because he could not put them in a novel.

In 1920, Pirandello announced that he was writing *Six Characters* as a play with the subtitle *commedia da fare in tre atti* (a play to be made in three acts). He dropped the last three words by the time the play was completed in 1921, insisting instead that the play should have neither acts nor scenes. In the 1925 preface, slightly modified from an essay titled "How and why I wrote *Six Characters,*"[5] the allegorical servant Fantasy re-appears, again presenting characters to the annoyed author. This time, Fantasy has dug up members of a troubled family who, she thinks, should be put into a novel. The author, however, realizes that these characters have become more independent than characters in a novel. "Detached from narrative support," they have become dramatic characters, and he decides to send them to a stage. Pirandello, then, still refuses to write either a narrative or a drama depicting the characters' situation, problems and conflicts. Instead, he writes a play about their failed attempt to create a drama, a "play to be made" that is never made. As he says in the preface, "[The characters] do not succeed in creating a drama precisely because the author that they are searching for is absent; what is staged instead is the comedy of their vain attempt with all its tragic content" (p. 22). Instead of drama, we have tragic content treated comically, the aesthetic mixture that Pirandello advocated in his 1908 essay "Umorismo" ("On Humor")[6] in which

5. "Come e perché ho scritto I 'Sei Personaggi'," published in *Comoedia* in January 1925. In Luigi Pirandello, *Saggi e interventi,* edited by Ferdinando Taviani (Milan: Mondadori, 2006), 1285–1300. Translated and published in *The Virginia Quarterly Review* (Spring 1925) as "Pirandello Confesses Why and How He Wrote *Six Characters in Search of an Author,*" http://www.vqronline.org/articles/1925/spring/pirandello-confesses/, accessed 29 June 2013.
6. Translated by Antonio Illiano and Daniel P. Testa, (Chapel Hill: University of North Carolina Press, 1974).

he defined "the feeling of the contrary" as the ability to laugh at and sympathize with a character, simultaneously.

The question of how the story should be told also appears in the conflict between the two main characters of the play. Basically, the Father wants to "tell" and the Stepdaughter wants to "show." The Father has a tendency to want to become a narrative author, attempting to explain his feelings and motivations in long-winded speeches. The Stepdaughter at one point interrupts him with "here you can't narrate!" *("qui non si narra")*, implying that onstage one must act, rather than recount. She, on the other hand, is "dying to play" the scene between them and also speaks, sings and dances like a performer. This conflict is to some extent both a battle for control of point of view and a battle of the sexes, but it may also be seen as internal to Pirandello as author. His characteristically long, literary stage directions seem like vestiges of a narrative he has not quite abandoned, supporting the dialogue and performance on the stage. The play's concern with the process of writing and staging a play, known as "metatheater," is thus central to its fabric.

Of course if *Six Characters* were only about the process of writing a play, it would not hold spectators' or readers' attention for very long. Within the conflict over the presentation of the story, however, lies a "terrible drama" involving an abandoned son, a mother who left her husband to have children with another man, including two who died and one who became a prostitute. This daughter encounters her stepfather as a client, later accusing him of causing all the disasters. The emotions expressed by the characters trying to convey their situation affect both the internal audience, composed of the theatrical company, and external audiences, all the more so because the details and the questions of blame are never quite clear. The story is gripping for another reason as well. The characters are portrayed not only as passionate human beings suffering from their family troubles, but also as unearthly creatures suffering from the fact that they are condemned to endure their condition eternally since they are not, like us, subject to change. In the nineteenth century, writers such as Eugène Scribe or Henrik Ibsen, by giving the illusion of reality, could have turned the characters' family situation into either a "well-made play" or a naturalistic drama, depicting real people living their lives behind the invisible fourth wall. In the twentieth century, Pirandello seems to be saying, such realistic representations are no longer possible.

Pirandello was, of course, not the first to question the conventions of nineteenth-century dramatic writing and staging. Contemporaries calling for the end of mimetic drama and the "retheatricalization" of theater — that is, treating the theater as theater and not as an imitation of life — included the Italian Futurists, led by Filippo Marinetti (1876–1944), and the Russian Nikolai Evreinov (1879–1953), both of whom had an impact on Pirandello. Marinetti claimed that Pirandello's conjuring of Madame Pace in Six Characters was influenced by him. The Futurists, flaunting both literary and theatrical conventions, produced what they called "syntheses" — poetic playlets about different events represented on stage simultaneously. Evreinov looked to European baroque theater — the *commedia dell'arte* as well as Lope de Vega, Cervantes and Shakespeare — to support his assault on the well-made play as well as on the naturalism of the Moscow Art Theater. He developed his notions of retheatricalization not only in his theoretical works, collected and published in English as *The Theatre in Life,* but also in his plays and his stage directing.

In 1921, as director of the Teatro d'Arte, Pirandello staged an Italian translation of Evreinov's metatheatrical *The Chief Thing.* As in *Six Characters,* the entire action of *The Chief Thing* takes place on a stage, during a rehearsal, with a director, actors and the prompter as characters. Evreinov, however, stresses his theory of theater more than Pirandello does. Human life, he claims, needs illusion more than reality, and the world will be saved by the actor and his magic art. Spectators need to be transported by such magic rather than looking at a banal imitation of life. If the skeptical Pirandello did not quite share Evreinov's idealistic belief in salvation through theatrical art, he did participate in his views on the importance of theatricality.

In spite of the contributions of Futurism and other experimental or avant-garde movements in early twentieth-century Italy, theater there at the time was overwhelmingly conservative.[7] The great actor or actress, who performed in an almost operatic fashion, was the center of attention more than the director or the author of the play. Many of the plays were of a melodramatic nature, "well-made" with a clear exposition, complications and resolution, often a

7. For a more complete description of Italian theater at the turn of the century, see Paolo Puppa, "The Theatre of United Italy," in Joseph Farrell and Paolo Puppa, eds., *A History of Italian Theatre* (Cambridge: Cambridge University Press, 2006), 223–34.

happy ending. With the impact of naturalist authors such as Ibsen, style and content began to change to a more natural, less operatic type of acting and an exploration of problems of real life with less emphasis on happy or moral resolutions. Still, the invisible "fourth wall" between stage and audience was strictly maintained in the theater. Before the establishment of cinema as the major vehicle for mass entertainment, the theater was extremely well-attended and important for the social life of the Italian bourgeoisie.

The composition of Italian theatrical troupes was also of a fixed, conservative nature — something that can be seen in the company represented in *Six Characters.* In France, Germany and elsewhere in Europe in the 1920s directors such as Georges Pitoëff and Max Reinhardt (known as *metteur-en-scène* in France and *Régisseur* in Germany) had a major impact on the conception and realization of how performances were staged. In Italy, however, there was not even a word for our contemporary notion of "director" until the 1930's, when the word *regista* was coined. The character whose function is translated as "director" here is in the original designated as *"il direttore-capocomico." "Capocomico"* means something like the head of the actors or the head of the theatrical company. One of his (they were always male) functions was indeed to direct, but in a limited way, and he was also what we would call today a managing director. The author was primary, the *capocomico* secondary in that the role of the latter was to help the actors to faithfully interpret and render the script of the former.

In a 1908 essay called "Illustrators, Actors, and Translators," Pirandello compares actors with translators in that the task of both is to attempt to transmit the original text as closely as possible — something they can never succeed in doing perfectly. Conceptions of actors', directors' and translators' roles have since evolved considerably. In Pirandello's case, as discussed above, his reception of the Pitoëff production as well as his own experience as *capocomico* led him to modify his position on the role of the director. In *Six Characters in Search of an Author,* however, the absence of an author is the primary reason that the *commedia da fare,* the play to be made, will not and cannot be created. The director in that play, a bit of a buffoon, deludes himself into thinking that he can substitute for the missing author. In Pirandello's final "theater in theater" play, *Tonight We Improvise,* "Dr. Hinkfuss," no longer a mere *capocomico* but a full-fledged *Régisseur,* tyrannizes the actors and distorts the text, imposing his own vision. Although he admired the work of Reinhardt and other new directors, Pirandello was also critical of what he saw as their excesses and sought to retain a balance between the powers of author and director.

The Italian theater troupe at the time was also strict in its definition of types of actors and what roles they played. In the theatrical company represented in *Six Characters* there is a lead actress, a lead actor, a second or supporting actress, a young actress or ingénue, a young actor and others. Conventional plays were usually designed so that the roles that each of these would play would be clear. Another actor often included in troupes was the *attore brillante* or comic actor. Others working in the company — stage manager, prop master, director's assistant and stagehands — had functions similar to those in theater today. The prompter, essential to play performances in Pirandello's time, is now only used, if at all, at the opera. As we see in the rehearsal in *Six Characters,* the prompter stood in a "box" under the stage, with a top on it, his head visible to the actors but presumably not to the audience. Following his copy of the script, he could mouth or whisper lines if a performer forgot them.

In this play set in a conventional early twentieth-century theater during a rehearsal, in broad daylight, Pirandello introduces two very different sets of characters in conflict with each other: on the one hand the personnel of the theater company, on the other the "characters," who arrive onstage through the auditorium to announce that they are "in search of an author." These are the very characters that were "born" to an author who was unable to put them into a novel but sent them out on their own to try the stage. One of them, the Son, refuses to act out his scenes, insisting that he is not a dramatic character. The Stepdaughter, on the other hand, as mentioned above, desperately wants to perform. The most talkative of them, the Father, who considers himself the group's spokesman, wants to substitute for the missing author, and in cooperation with the Director, to create a play. The Mother, who does not have the intellectual awareness of the others, lives and suffers as a character — eternally — because her situation will never change. The two young children never speak, because they are dead. The characters are both shocked and amused by the actors' attempts to play them. How can an actor ever "be" a character? The Father and the Stepdaughter conjure up a seventh character, the seamstress and brothel owner Madame Pace, because she is needed for the scene they must play. For the actors, her appearance must be some sort of cheap trick; for the characters, it is part of their reality. Although the actors begin to sympathize with the characters' "terrible drama," the chasm between the two groups is never bridged. The actors, like other ordinary people who play their parts and change from one moment to the next are "real"; the characters, which do not change, are "true." The question, remains, however, of who these characters are. Ghost-like creatures? Figments of the imagination that resemble, but are not, human beings?

As mentioned above, the Stepdaughter, one of the two most prominent characters, is also something of a performer. A "fallen woman" in the language of the day, only eighteen years old, she is unique among Pirandello's creations in that she actually sings and dances onstage. The song that she sings, "Chou Chin Chow," was composed by Dave Stamper, with lyrics by Gene Buck, both Americans, for the Ziegfeld Follies of 1917. It was then arranged by Francis Salabert, with lyrics in French by Lucien Boyer, as "Prends garde à Tchou-Tchin-Tchou" ("Beware of Chou-Chin-Chow"). It is this version, whose words differ from the English one, that she sings. The music and lyrics in both English and French are printed in the appendix here. The character Chou-Chin-Chow appears to be an imaginary Chinese version of Ali Baba of the forty thieves, also a "Chinese Romeo." There seems to be no particular reason why Pirandello picked this song except that it was popular at the time and gives the Stepdaughter an opportunity to act like a Ziegfeld Follies girl.

Pirandello's most famous play has been translated into English several times, beginning with Edward Storer's *Six Characters in Search of an Author: A Comedy in the Making* in 1922. Anyone translating from Italian must face the intimidating Italian pun *traduttore/traditore*: the translator is a traitor. Translating Pirandello, we must also remember his essay on translators and actors in which he argues that both necessarily produce a text inferior to the original. Indeed, if the primary goal of the translator is to be "faithful" to the original, the endeavor is doomed to failure, since no language can ever replicate exactly the shades of meaning, sounds and cultural connotations of another. It may be argued, however, that translations can also lead to new cultural connotations and meanings. The German theorist Walter Benjamin, in an essay published in 1923, translated as "The Task of the Translator," opened up new ways of thinking about translation with his observation that the translator is responsible for the "afterlife" of a work, renewing and transforming it. For this reason, no translation is ever definitive, for the process of renewal is ongoing. Contemporary translation theories tend to emphasize the similarities between translation and interpretation, and the fact that the translator is responsible for transmitting a text from one culture to another. Yet the linguistic dilemmas remain. Translating for the theater poses its own special problems. Pirandello's wordy, long, and complex sentences, particularly those pronounced by the Father, fit the Italian stage but are not easily transformed into readable or actable English. We have chosen in many instances to break such speeches into shorter sentences, conforming more closely to contemporary American usage. Madame Pace, in the original, speaks a combination of Italian and Spanish; we have rendered this as a combination of English and Spanish.

Another challenge in translating the speech of the characters lies in the fact that their otherness or strangeness must be maintained. They will never become our next-door neighbors, and they should not sound or act as if they were. The structure of the Italian theater company and the nature of the Italian stage in the 1920s also pose problems. A contemporary director might choose to alter the text to do away with the prompter, for example, and to modernize the company. Here we have chosen to retain the company as it was, hoping to bring out Pirandello's criticism of the theater of his time contrasted with the revolutionary nature of his play. Our aim, ambitious as it might be, is to reveal Pirandello as both accessible and fascinating for contemporary readers, actors and audiences, and to contribute to his afterlife.

Mary Ann Frese Witt

CHARACTERS[1]

I'm holding an audience today. From nine to twelve this morning I shall receive in my study the ladies and gentlemen of my future stories.

What personalities!

I don't know why all these people, dissatisfied with their lives, betrayed by fate, the mocked, the disillusioned, the half-crazy, must come to *me*. If I treated them well, I would understand. But generally I treat them like dogs. They know I'm hard to please. I'm cruelly curious, and I don't let myself be fooled by appearances or duped by chitchat. For God's sake, I even demand proofs, evidence and documents from some of them. And yet, they all have — or think they have (it's really the same thing) — their own problems that they want to make known, and they come to me insistently begging for a voice and a life.

"What for?" I say to them. There are already too many of us here in this sordid, real world, claiming the right to live, my dear friends. This life could be easy (vain and stupid as it is), if we didn't fiercely and zealously make it more difficult day by day. Cursedly, we complicate it with newfangled inventions and discoveries, which seem to make it easier and more comfortable for us, perhaps just to hide from our own eyes the stupid and awful vanity. You, my friends, have the good fortune to be empty shadows. Why do you, too, want to take on life at my expense? And what sort of life would it be as the poor inhabitants of an emptier world, a miserable paper world in which, I assure you, life is joyless? Look here: everything in this paper world is rigged, engineered, adapted to the ends that the writer, a little Eternal Father, thinks up for himself.

There are never any of those unexpected obstacles that, in reality, gracefully thwart and limit and modify the characteristics of individuals and life. Nature (lucky nature!), with no apparent order, happily bristling with contradictions, is — believe me — far, far away from these tiny artificial worlds where the elements appear to hold together and cooperate. Concentrated life, simplified life, without true reality. In reality, don't actions that bring out character define themselves against a background of ordinary events, of

1. Originally published as "Personaggi" in *Il Ventesimo,* June 10, 1906; republished in Mario Costanzo, ed., *Novelle per un anno,* 3.2 (Milan: Mondadori, 1990), 1474–78.

common details? Well then, writers don't take advantage of this, as if these events, these details, were useless and without value. In nature, isn't gold mixed with earth? Well, writers throw away the earth and present the gold — refined, melted down, precisely weighed — in new coins stamped with their brand and crest. But don't ordinary events and common details — the materiality of life, so varied and complex — bitterly contradict those artificial simplifications? Don't those ordinary events cause actions and inspire thoughts and feelings contrary to that harmonious logic of facts and characteristics as conceived by writers? And the unforeseen in life? The abyss in the soul?

By God, don't I feel strange thoughts swarming inside me, almost flashes of madness, incoherent and unmentionable, as if coming from a soul different from the one I usually recognize in myself? And how many unforeseen and unforeseeable occasions arise in life, like improvised hooks that seize souls in a fleeting moment — a moment of pettiness or generosity, noble or shameful? Those souls keep hanging, either on the altar or the pillory, for their entire existence, as though everything were summed up in that moment alone, that moment of passing exhilaration or loss of control. The business of art, my friends, is to immobilize souls, to fix life in one or several determining moments: a statue in a gesture; a landscape in a temporary, unchangeable glimpse. But what torture! What about the perpetual mobility of what follows? And the continuous fusion of souls?

This is how I speak to the ladies and gentlemen who are my characters. Indeed! As though I were speaking to the wall.

And then, to get them out of my way, to escape from their mute, oppressive siege, I start to listen to them. Ah, what lowlives! After I've given them my blood, my life, and I've felt their pains as my own, their misadventures — yes indeed! As soon as they leave my study, they go around saying that I'm a sardonic writer and that instead of making people cry over their misery, I make them laugh, etc., etc.

Above all, they can't stand my precise descriptions of certain little physical or moral defects of theirs. They'd all like to be good-looking, my noble characters, and morally impeccable. Miserable, yes, but beautiful. Think about that!

Now, we come to the audience. I have a little maid, who, although she dresses in black and reads philosophy books whenever she can (each to her own taste!), laughs a lot and runs around like a crazy girl. Oh, and some of her laughter reminds me of acrobatics that an urchin might perform with a band. In case anyone is curious, my servant's name is Fantasy. I suspect that, just to annoy me, she secretly goes out to look for and dig up all these lovely creatures that present themselves to me. And another thing. I told her a thousand times that she is supposed to usher them into my study one by one. But no! They come all together, in flocks, so that I don't know which ones to listen to first.

Today, for example, a boy riding a stick leapt into my study, where he began to kick up a fuss: laughing, running, screaming, knocking down all my chairs. "Fantasy! Fantasy!" I cry. An old English nursemaid comes in, skinny, dried up, stiff, dressed like a nun in gray, with horn-rimmed glasses and a white cap on her stringy hair. She begins to run after the boy, who slips out of her hands and can't be caught. In the meantime, Fantasy is whispering in my ear that the boy, so lively and cheerful, has a very sad story. That stick he's riding like a horse belongs to his mother's lover, and I don't know what else she tells me.

"All right!" I cry to her. "But for now get rid of him! How am I supposed to pay attention to the others with him here? And who's that little old man over there, blind, dressed in rags, with a rosary in his hand? Get rid of him, too! And also those giddy girls surrounding him."

"Quiet, for pity's sake! They are his daughters...."

"Well?"

"He doesn't know what's going on. He can't see. He's a pious man, but his daughters...there, in his house (what a house, if you could see it!), while he's saying his rosary...."

"I want nothing to do with them," I scream. "Get rid of them! These are old stories. I don't have time to waste with them. Let me listen to this gentleman who, at least, is well-dressed."

The man is well-dressed to an extent, anyway. He's wearing a long coat, open in the front, on which it seems that the tailor forgot to sew the tails. He smiles at me, bows, and lightly touches two fingers to his waxed mustache. What a mustache! It looks like two mice squatting under his nose with their tails uplifted. He looks about forty, dark-skinned, bald and with deep black eyes alongside his powerful nose. (He will also claim that he should be portrayed as handsome!)

Sit down," I say to him. "For heaven's sake, stop touching your mustache. Don't mess it up, or I'll take it away from you. First of all, let's establish your name. What do you want to be called?"

"If you don't mind, at your command, I would like to be called Leandro," he answers me with a little spider's voice as he stands up and bows again. "And for my last name, if you don't mind, Scoto."

"Leandro Scoto? Let's see. Stand over there, like that. That's enough. Now turn around. Yes, it seems to me the name suits you. Leandro Scoto it is."

"And — Doctor?" the little man adds timidly, smiling again. "If you don't mind, I would like to be 'Doctor.'"

"Doctor of what?" I ask, looking him up and down.

"If you don't mind...."

I can't stand it anymore, so I burst out: "Just stop with the 'if you don't mind' once and for all! Say what you mean."

"Well then, by your leave," he responds, mortified, looking down at his long and well-manicured fingernails, "Doctor of physical and mathematical sciences."

"Hmm," I say. "It seems to me that you look more like a provincial notary or a head archivist. But let's go on. So, you'll be called *Leandro Scoto, Doctor of physical and mathematical sciences.* You have a book with you? What is it? Come closer."

Doctor Leandro Scoto draws near to me and, with some hesitation, hands me the book. "It's in English," he says with lowered eyes. "A book by Leadbeater."[2]

"The theosophist?" I exclaim. "Ah, I don't want anything to do with it, you know. Go away! If you're coming here to be considered with books like that, you can just leave. I've already put a theosophist into one of my novels, and that's enough. I know how much work it was to keep him from seeming a bore! Enough, enough."

"No, I was saying...," Doctor Leandro Scoto risks with a pleading look.

"I tell you that's enough!" I yell at him again in a peremptory tone. "I am amazed that a doctor in physical and mathematical sciences, such as you claim to be, thus a serious man, can be interested in such meaningless trivialities."

2. Charles Webster Leadbeater (1854–1934) was an official of the British Theosophical Society, a spiritualist and occult movement. His conception of character had an influence on Pirandello.

Deeply saddened, Doctor Leandro Scoto stands up for the third time and bows for the third time, one hand on his chest.

"Pardon me," he says. "If you want nothing to do with me, I can go away. Disappear. But don't judge me in such a superficial manner. *I'm* not a theosophist. Today, we all feel the need to believe in something. Illusions are absolutely necessary, and science, as you well know, cannot give them to us. Thus I, too, have read a few books on theosophy. Believe me, I laughed over them. Oh, aberrations, aberrations.... And yet, look! In this book I found a most curious passage — a certain idea that seems to me to have some basis in truth and that could interest you very much. Will you allow me?"

He sits next to me, opens the book to page 104 and begins to read, translating correctly from English: "We have said that the *elemental* essence that surrounds it from every side is especially subject, in all its varieties, to the action of human thought. We have described that which produces on it the passage of the slightest errant thought, that is to say the sudden formation of a diaphanous nephelometry whose forms are continuously moving and changing. Now we will say what happens when the human spirit positively expresses a precise thought or desire. The thought assumes a plastic essence. It plunges into it, so to speak, and instantly models itself in the form of a living being that appears to be taking on the quality of thought itself, and this being, barely formed, is no longer at all under the control of its creator, but enjoys its own life, whose length is relative to the intensity of the thought and the desire that generated it. In fact, it lasts according to the strength of the thought that holds the parts together."

Doctor Leandro Scoto closes the book and looks at me. "Well then," he adds, "no one can know better than you that this is true. And I, insofar as I am not yet free and independent from you, am proof of this. All characters created by art are proof of this. Some unfortunately have an ephemeral life; others an immortal one. A true life, more true than the real one, I would say! Angelica, Rodomonte, Shylock, Hamlet, Juliet, Don Quixote, Manon Lescaut, Don Abbondio, Tartarin[3]: don't they live an indestructible life, a life by now independent of their authors?"

3. All literary characters: Angelica and Rodomonte in both *Orlando innamorato* by Boiardo and *Orlando furioso* by Ariosto; Shylock, Hamlet and Juliet in plays by Shakespeare; Don Quixote in the eponymous novel

In turn, I look at Doctor Leandro Scoto, who has shown himself to be so erudite, and I ask him, "Excuse me, exactly where are you going with this theosophical-aesthetic dissertation?"

"Into life!" he exclaims, with a melodramatic gesture. "I want to live. I have a great desire to live; for my happiness and that of others. Let me live, sir! Let me live well, I beg you. You can see I have a good heart! I'm intelligent enough. I have good intentions and modest desires. I deserve good fortune. Please grant me an imperishable existence."

I can't stand presumptuous people. I stare at him, eye to eye, and then I look at his feet, as if to make him move away, and I say to him, "Now come on, little doctor, are you serious? What is there in you that deserves immortality?"

"Oh, I'm not presuming, I'm not presuming anything," Doctor Leandro Scoto hastens to answer me, stepping back with his hands on his chest. "Excuse me. It doesn't depend on me. It depends on you. I might just as well be a fool, what does it matter? Consider, for example, Don Abbondio.[4] God almighty, who is he? An ordinary little village priest, a frightened little soul, and — yes, sir! — what good fortune that character has had. He lives eternally! You can have me commit some atrocity or, perhaps confront death to save a fellow human being or do a good turn to a friend to deserve his gratitude or even let me take a wife — what can I say? — with the promise of living happily and peacefully, but for heaven's sake, don't abandon me! Give me life. Make use of me. Have faith that, if you reach into my depths, you will find in me the material for a masterpiece."

Oof! I can no longer contain myself. I jump to my feet. "Dear Doctor Leandro Scoto," I tell him, "listen. For the masterpiece, come back tomorrow."

---

by Cervantes; Manon Lescaut in the eponymous novel by Prévost and opera by Puccini; Don Abbondio in Alessandro Manzoni's novel *I promessi sposi (The Betrothed);* and Tartarin in a series of novels with his name in each title by Alphonse Daudet.

4. He is mentioned in a similar speech by the Father in *Six Characters in Search of an Author.*

The Tragedy of a Character[1]

It is an old habit of mine to hold an audience every Sunday morning for the characters of my future short stories. For five hours, from eight am to one pm. It almost always happens that I find myself in bad company.

I do not know why: usually those attending my audiences are the unhappiest people in the world, afflicted with strange diseases or entangled in the most incredible situations, people who are really hard to deal with.

I listen to them all with great tolerance. I question them with courtesy. I take note of their names and situations; I consider the feelings and aspirations of each. But I must add that to my disgrace, by nature, I am not easily pleased. Tolerance, courtesy, yes, but I do not appreciate being tricked. And I would like to plunge the depths of their souls with a long and detailed investigation.

It does happen that, in response to some of my questions, they dig in their heels and take shelter, furiously resisting, perhaps because they think I enjoy making fun of their seriousness.

Patiently and courteously I try to prove to them that my question was not superfluous, because it is easy for a person to *desire* to be one way or another. The question hinges on whether we *can* be the way we want. When the power to do so is lacking, the desire seems ridiculous and vain.

They refuse to be persuaded.

I, who am fundamentally good hearted, feel sorry for them. But is it possible to feel sorry for certain misfortunes without being simultaneously able to laugh at them? Well, the characters from my short stories go around spreading the word that I am a cruel and heartless writer. Only a well-disposed critic can show how much sympathy underlies that laughter.

But where are the well-disposed critics?

I must point out that certain characters in these audiences jump in front of the others, making themselves known with such petulance and self-importance that I sometimes find myself forced to allow them to live right away.

Later many of them bitterly regret such impatience and beg me to fix one defect or another. But I smile and tell them that they must

1. First published in *Corriere della sera,* December 17, 1911.

now atone for their original sin and wait until the crowd around me has dispersed, and I have the time and means to get back to them.

Among those who stay behind, waiting, overwhelmed, a few sigh, a few grow sullen, a few grow tired and go off to knock on some other writer's door. On occasion I have found in the stories written by colleagues of mine characters who came to me first. I have also recognized others who — dissatisfied with how I have treated them — decided to go elsewhere to try and cut a better figure.

I don't complain because about once a week two or three new ones come to see me, joining the hardly small number of those already waiting. Often the crowd is so large that I must listen to more than one at the same time. But at a certain point, my mind becomes so distracted and overrun that it refuses that double or triple nourishing and cries out in exasperation, "Either come to me calmly and quietly, one at a time, or I call the whole thing off for all three of you."

I still remember how submissively a poor, old man who had come from afar waited. He was a maestro named Icilio Saporini, who had emigrated to America in 1849 after the fall of the Roman Republic because he had composed the music for a patriotic anthem. After forty-five years, at almost eighty years old, he had returned to Italy to die. Ceremonious, and in his little mosquito voice, he let everyone skip ahead of him. And finally one day while convalescing after a long illness, I saw him enter the room, very humble, with a shy little smile on his lips:"If I may...if you don't mind...."

"Oh, yes, my dear old man!" He had chosen the most opportune moment, and I had him die right away in a little story called "Old Music."

This last Sunday I was a little later than usual entering the study for my audience.

A long novel, sent to me as a gift, had been waiting over a month to be read. It had kept me up until three in the morning because of the many reflections one of the characters had inspired in me, the only one alive in a crowd of empty shadows. The character was an unfortunate man, a certain Doctor Fileno, who believed he'd found an infallible remedy for every kind of ailment, a cure-all for every private and public disaster.

In actuality, more than a remedy or a cure-all, Doctor Fileno's discovery was a method that consisted of reading history books from morning until evening and viewing the present as history as well, as though the present were already remote and filed in the archives of the past.

With this method, he had freed himself of all pain and worry, and he had found — without needing to die — peace: an austere and serene peace, permeated with that melancholy free of regret, which will be preserved in every cemetery on earth even when people cease to exist.

Doctor Fileno did not even dream of using the past to derive lessons for the present. He knew it would be a waste of time and a game for fools; because history is the composite of elements gathered according to the nature, dislikes, likes, aspirations and opinions of historians, and it is thus impossible to apply this composite to life, which proceeds with its elements separate and scattered. And he did not even dream of deriving from the present norms or forecasts for the future; in fact, the opposite was true. He cast himself in the future in order to look back on the present, which he viewed as past.

For example, a few days earlier, his daughter had died. A friend had gone to console him in his misery, but he found him already consoled, as though his daughter had died over a hundred years ago.

He had taken his misfortune, still so fresh, had distanced it in time, relegating it to the past. It was with such perspective and dignity that he spoke of his daughter's death. In brief, using his method, Dr. Fileno had created something resembling a telescope in reverse. He did not use it to look towards the future where he knew he wouldn't see anything; he consoled himself by looking from the larger lens through the small one, which pointed toward the present so that everything there would suddenly appear small and far away. And he had been waiting for several years to compose a book, which certainly would have caused a sensation: *The Philosophy of Distance.* While I was reading the novel, it became clear to me that the author, completely intent on artificially weaving together one of the most standard plots, had not been able to conceptualize this character. Containing the seed of a true and proper creation, he had seized the author's hand and made himself stand out from a trite narrative. Then suddenly, deformed and weakened, Dr. Fileno had allowed himself to adapt to the demands of a false and silly conclusion.

I stayed for a long time in the night's silence with that character before my eyes, reflecting. What a shame! There was enough raw material in him to produce a masterpiece. Had the author not so undeservingly misunderstood and neglected him, had he made Dr. Fileno the center of his narrative, even all those artificial elements he had used would suddenly have come alive. A great sorrow and resentment took hold of me for the poor life that might have been.

That morning, entering my study late, I found an unusual disorder because Dr. Fileno had already pushed his way into the crowd of characters waiting who, angry and annoyed, had jumped on him and were trying to chase him out and pull him back. "Hey," I yelled, "ladies and gentlemen, is this any way to behave? Dr. Fileno, I have already wasted too much time with you. What do you want from me? You don't belong to me. Let me attend to my characters in peace now and go away. Such an intense and desperate despair appeared on Dr. Fileno's face that instantly all those others — my characters who were still trying to restrain him — grew pale with shame and drew back. "Don't chase me away, don't chase me away! Just listen to me for five minutes, with the permission of these ladies and gentlemen, and let me persuade you, please."

"Persuade me of what? I am completely persuaded that you, my dear doctor, deserve to fall into better hands. But what do you want me to do for you? I have already grieved over your fate. Now that's enough."

"Enough? Oh, no, by God," Dr. Fileno burst out, his body shuddering with indignation. "You say that only because I am not your creation. Your neglect, your disdain, would be — believe me — much less cruel than this passive pity unworthy of an artist. My apologies. No one knows better than you that we are live beings, more alive than those who breathe and wear clothes; perhaps less real but more true. One is born in so many ways, my dear sir, and you know very well that nature uses the instrument of human imagination to carry out its creative work. And whoever is born thanks to this creative activity situated in the human spirit is destined by nature to a life far superior to that of those born from a woman's mortal womb. Whoever is born a character, whoever has the good fortune to be born a living character can even scoff at death. He will never die! The man will die, the writer, the natural instrument of creation. The creation will never die! And in order to live forever, a character doesn't even need to be a genius or to work wonders. Tell me, who was Sancho Panza! Tell me, who was Don

Abbondio![2] And yet they live forever because as living embryos they had the good fortune to find a fertile womb, an imagination that was able to nurture them and help them grow for eternity.

"Of course, my dear doctor, that's all well and good," I said to him, "but I still don't see what you could possibly want from me."

"Oh no, you don't see?" asked Dr. Fileno. "Have I lost my way? Have I accidentally landed on the moon? Excuse me, but what kind of writer are you? Do you seriously not understand the horror of my tragedy? To have the incomparable privilege of being born a character, now that material life is so bristling with petty difficulties that block, deform and impoverish existence; what a privilege to be born a living character, thus destined, insignificant as I am, to immortality. But to have fallen into those hands — yes sir — condemned to perish unjustly, to suffocate in this artificial world where I can neither draw a breath nor take a single step because it is all fictitious, contrived, convoluted! Words and paper! Paper and words! If a man finds himself entangled in circumstances to which he cannot or does not know how to adapt, he can escape from them, run away; a poor character cannot. He is stuck there, nailed to endless martyrdom. Air! Air! Life! Look here...*Fileno*...he gave me the name 'Fileno.' Do you seriously think that 'Fileno' can be my name? Imbecile, imbecile. He couldn't even properly name me. I, Fileno, and then I, author of *The Philosophy of Distance*, I of all people had to end up in that unworthy situation in order to unravel that whole stupid mess of events. Did I, rather than the Notary Negroni, actually have to marry that harebrained Graziella in a second marriage? Be serious! These are crimes, my dear sir, crimes that must be paid for with tears of blood. But now what? What will happen? Nothing. Silence. A few critical remarks in two or three minor journals. Maybe some critic will exclaim, 'Poor Dr. Fileno. What a shame. That one was a good character!' And it will all end like that. Condemned to death, I, the author of *The Philosophy of Distance*, which that imbecile wasn't even able to have me publish, even at my own expense! I challenge you to tell me how I could have made a second marriage with that harebrained Graziella. Oh, don't make me think about it. Come, come, get to work, my dear sir. Redeem me at once, at once. You have clearly understood the

2. The former is a character in Cervantes' *Don Quixote*; the latter a character in Alessandro Manzoni's *I promessi sposi (The Betrothed)*, a novel published in final form in 1842 and well-known to Italians.

life that's in me; so let me live." As I heard this proposal, let out in fury as the conclusion to his long outburst, I remained befuddled awhile, staring at Dr. Fileno.

"Do you have qualms?" he asked me, becoming upset. "Do you have qualms? It is perfectly legitimate, you know. It is your sacrosanct right to take me in and give me the life that that imbecile was unable to give me. It is your right and mine. Do you understand?"

"Maybe it's your right, dear doctor, and it may even be legitimate as you believe, but I won't do such things, and there's no use insisting. I won't do it. Try appealing to someone else."

"And to whom do you suggest that I appeal if you. . . ."

"I don't know! Try. Maybe it won't take much to find someone completely convinced that this right of yours is legitimate. If not, please listen to me, Dr. Fileno: Are you or are you not truly the author of *The Philosophy of Distance*?"

"Of course," snapped Dr. Fileno, taking a step backwards, putting his hands on his chest, "Would you dare to doubt it? As usual, it is the fault of my murderer. He barely sketched out my theories, not understanding in the slightest all the benefits that could be derived from my discovery of the reversed telescope."

I held up my hands to stop him, smiling and saying, "All right, all right, but what about you?"

"What *about* me?"

"You complain about your author but have you been able, my dear doctor, to benefit from your theory?"

"This is precisely what I wanted to tell you."

"Let me speak. If you seriously believe as I do in the worthiness of your philosophy, why don't you apply it to your case? You are presently in search of an author who will consecrate you to immortality, but look at what all the most highly regarded critics say about us miserable little contemporary writers. We are and we aren't, my dear doctor. Use your reverse telescope to examine us together with the most notable facts, the most burning questions and the most admired works of our days. My dear doctor, I am very much afraid that you'll see nothing and no one. So cheer up, or resign yourself and let me attend to my poor characters who — nasty and difficult though they may be — at least don't have your extravagant ambition.

Fragment from *Six Characters in Search of an Author: A Novel to be Made*[1]

These girls and their hour! Signora Pace told him that one had insisted she really could come only between three and four in the afternoon and stay only for that hour, not one minute more, not one minute less, because she was going to school, her third year of high school. She would be at school until three, and after four she needed to do her homework so that at seven she could accompany Mamma for a ride in her carriage to the Pincio Gardens.[2]

A building like many others, five stories, in one of the city's new and most popular streets. On the first floor, the offices of a bank; on the second, the rooms of one of the cleanest "bed and breakfasts for families." The four inches of gold stripes on the doorman's hat attested to the respectability of all the inhabitants, even those on the fifth floor.

And yet, every time he caught sight of the doorman from afar, he felt humiliated by a burning sense of shame, as though all the passers-by would read in his face his intention to enter the building and ascend to the floor where a certain Signora Pace, under the rigorously observed appearance of a *Tailleuse pour dames*, practiced for the benefit of her chosen clients (and perhaps also for their husbands) another profession, a rather common one in large cities.

He could not see himself as others on the street saw him — a passer-by like any other, unknown, tall, fat, well-dressed, around fifty years old, among many other anonymous people, more or less well-dressed. He knew himself, though. The street brought everything with it, crowded as it was with pedestrians, so it was as though that street and all those pedestrians entered that door with him.

Contrary to his external appearance as an elderly gentleman, internally, he felt the grotesque shriek of a shameless desire that would — in a little while — shoo him through that entranceway.

---

1. 'I sei personaggi,' in "Foglietti," Corrado Alvaro, ed. 1934, in Luigi Pirandello, *Saggi, Poesie, Scritti Varii* (Milan: Mondadori, 1977) 1256–58.
2. Located on the Pincian Hill in Rome, near the Villa Borghese.

He watched the irreducible core of youth inside him, hidden beneath the serious appearance of an old man, going down the street in brutal, wild nudity. He should have been in the middle of the woods, but instead all around him he saw the city, clean and sparkling with windows. And then, little by little, his eyes, already shining, hardened. As his temples purpled, becoming almost black near his large buzzing ears, a convulsive tightening transmitted an almost cat-like convulsive shudder on his left cheek and nostril, and his mouth stretched into a sort of vulgar sneer. He stared at the passers-by with those shining, hard eyes, sneering in reaction to his shame. He did not hear the estranged conversations, the greetings that the passers-by exchanged with each other while walking, the screeching of the wheels on the tracks, the humming, the ringing of the electric trolley's bells, the shouts of street vendors and news agents. All that usual, daily, noisy movement of the street was, for him, a confusion, which he had to tear off in blind violence in order to get through that doorway. There, he went through it. The electric trolleys continued to screech on the tracks, ringing their bells; the street vendors continued to yell about their merchandise, the news agents about their newspapers; all the passers-by continued their conversations. He, meanwhile, climbing the stairs in that building with fierce, frantic sadness, trembled all over from the effort with which — almost on fire — he had severed himself from the hubbub of the street.

The best thing is this: they have left me and among themselves have begun to act out the scenes of this novel, just as those scenes should be. They act them out in front of me but as though I were not there, as though they did not depend on me, as though I can in no way interfere.

Especially her — the girl. I see her enter. She is a perfect reality created by me, but who doesn't interest me, though I feel the deep pity she inspires. The case of the mother. Imagine! Her shame before her legitimate son: she is unable to look at him because to look at him means she must deny the life of the other children who are the children of her suffering and her shame, of another life that he cannot enter.

Excerpt from a Letter[1]

From Luigi Pirandello to his son Stefano, who was a prisoner of war in Mathausen, dated July 23, 1917.

But I already have my head full of new things! So many stories… and something very strange and sad, so sad. *Six Characters in Search of an Author: A Novel to Be Made*. Maybe you will understand. Six characters, caught in a terrible drama, come to me, asking to be put into a novel — an obsession. I don't want to have anything to do with them, and I tell them that it's useless and that I don't care about them and no longer care about anything, and they show me all of their wounds. I shoo them all away…and thus in the end the whole novel to be made will be written.

1. In Andrea Pirandello, ed., *Il figlio prisioniero: Carteggio tra Luigi e Stefano Pirandello durante la Guerra 1915–1918* (Milan: Mondadori, 2005), 214–15.

Preface to *Six Characters*[1]

Though it seems like she just arrived, my clever little maid, who always acts like she's new to the job, has been in service to my art for many years. Her name is Fantasy.

She's mischievous and sarcastic and likes to dress in black, but there's no doubt that she's often eccentric, and no one can believe that she does everything seriously and routinely. She sticks her hand in her pocket, pulls out and puts on her head a fool's cap, red as a cockscomb, with bells, and off she goes. Here today. There tomorrow. And she enjoys bringing me — as fodder for stories, novels and plays — the most discontented people in the world. They are men, women and children involved in strange situations from which they can find no way out — thwarted in their plans, cheated in their hopes — and real thorns in the side.

Well then, this little servant of mine, Fantasy, several years ago now, on an ill-fated whim, brought home to me an entire family — I have no idea where or how she dug them up. In her opinion, I could create a magnificent novel with them.

I found myself facing a man of about fifty, wearing a black jacket and light-colored pants, frowning, his eyes sullen with mortification; a poor woman in widow's weeds holding the hand of a little four-year-old girl on one side and of a boy around ten on the other. With them and also dressed in black, but with suggestive and brash opulence, strode an impudent and provocative young woman. She was shaking all over with a kind of gleeful, biting contempt for that mortified old man as well as for a young man of about twenty who stood apart from the others, keeping to himself, as though he held them all in contempt. In other words, they were the six characters who come onstage at the beginning of this play. And then one or the other — often one drowning out the other — began to tell me their sad stories, shouting and hurling in my face their messy passions, more or less as they do to the unfortunate Director in the play.

What author could ever say how and why his imagination gives birth to a character? The mystery of artistic creation is the same as

1. "Prefazione" to *Sei personaggi in cerca d'autore: Commedia da fare*, in Luigi Pirandello, *Maschere Nude,* vol. 2, edited by Alessandro d'Amico (Milan: Mondadori, 2001), 653–67.

the mystery of natural birth. A woman, while making love, may desire to become a mother, but the desire alone, intense as it may be, is not enough. One fine day she finds herself a mother, not knowing exactly when it happened. In the same way, an artist, during his life, gathers into himself innumerable living seeds and can never explain how or why, at a certain moment, one of those vital seeds inserts itself into his imagination to become a living creature existing on a level superior to our capricious everyday existence.

All I can say is that, without being at all aware of ever seeking them, I found myself facing — so alive I could touch them, so alive I could even hear them breathing — those six characters that now can be seen onstage. There they were, each with a secret torment but united by birth and by a tangle of common issues. They were waiting for me to usher them into the world of art by composing from their persons, their passions and their cases a novel, a drama or at least a story.

Born alive, they wanted to live.

I would like to make it clear that, for me, it was never enough to portray the figure of a man or a woman, no matter how special and characteristic, just for the pleasure of portrayal or to narrate an event, happy or sad, just for the pleasure of narration or to describe a landscape just for the pleasure of description. There are of course writers (they are not few) who take such pleasures and, once satisfied, look no further. They are writers of a more historical nature. But there are others who, in addition to that sort of pleasure, feel a deeper spiritual need, which does not allow them to admit into the narrative figures, events or landscapes that are not imbued, so to speak, with a distinct sense of life, which gives them a universal value. These are writers of a more philosophical nature. I have the misfortune of belonging to the latter group.

I hate symbolic art, in which representation loses all its spontaneity to become mechanical and allegorical — a vain and misguided effort. Giving an allegorical meaning makes what is being represented seem neither imaginary nor real, but rather constructed in order to demonstrate some kind of moral truth. The spiritual need I speak of cannot be satisfied by such allegorical symbolism, except occasionally for the purpose of achieving a superior irony, as for example in Ariosto.[2] The symbolism derives from a concept, which becomes, or attempts to become, an image. Philosophical writing, on the other hand, seeks in the image, which must remain alive and free in every aspect of its expression, a meaning that will give it value.

Now, no matter how hard I tried, I was not able to discover such a meaning in those six characters. I therefore decided that it was not worth making them live. I thought to myself, "I have already afflicted my readers with hundreds and hundreds of stories. Why should I bother them further by telling the sad stories of these six miserable wretches?" Thinking along those lines, I sent them away. Or rather, I tried my best to send them away.

But one doesn't give life to a character for nothing. Creations of my mind, those six were already living a life that was their own and no longer mine, a life that I had no power to deny them.

In fact, while I kept trying to drive them out of my mind, they continued to live on their own. They had already detached themselves from any narrative support, miraculously able to step out of the pages of the novel that contained them. They chose certain moments of the day to confront me in the solitude of my study. Now one, now another, sometimes two together, they would come to tempt me, suggesting that I show or describe this or that scene, pointing out the effects that could result from these scenes or the new interest that a certain unusual situation might arouse and so on.

For a moment, I let myself be convinced, and every time I agreed or allowed myself to be taken in, they'd take advantage of it, finding more evidence to persuade me to allow them to live. And thus, little by little, it became as difficult for me to go back to freeing myself from them as it was easy for them to return to tempting me. At a certain point, I was truly obsessed by them. Until, suddenly, the way out flashed through my mind.

"Why don't I," I said to myself, "depict this unprecedented situation of an author who refuses to allow certain characters, born alive from his imagination, to live? And what if these characters, infused with life, refuse to resign themselves to remaining excluded from the world of art? They are already detached from me and

---

2. Ludovico Ariosto (September 8, 1474 – July 6, 1533) was a poet from the Reggio Emilia region of Italy. He is best known as the author of the 1516 romance epic *Orlando Furioso.*

living their own lives. They speak and move. Through the struggle for life that they have had to persist in with me, they have become dramatic characters, characters able to move and speak on their own — they already see themselves as such. They have learned how to defend themselves against me; they'll be able to defend themselves against others. So then, let's let them go where dramatic characters usually go to live: on a stage. And let's wait and see what happens.

That's just what I did. And naturally what was bound to happen did happen. The result was a mixture of the tragic and the comic, the fantastic and the realistic, in a completely new and infinitely complex "humoristic"[3] situation: a drama that by itself, by means of its breathing, speaking, self-propelled characters, who carry it and suffer it in themselves, demands to be staged at any cost, along with the comedy of the vain attempt to improvise this onstage realization. First comes the surprise of the poor actors in a theater company who are, during the day, rehearsing a play on a stage devoid of scenery and wings: surprise and disbelief when those six characters appear before them, declaring themselves to be in search of an author. Immediately following this, the Mother, veiled in black, suddenly faints, sparking the actors' instinctive interest as they perceive in her, and in the other members of that strange family, an obscure, ambiguous drama, which then comes unwittingly crashing down on that empty stage so unprepared to receive it. Little by little, interest deepens in the outburst of contrasting emotions from the Father, the Stepdaughter, the Son and from that poor Mother — emotions that attempt, as mentioned, to overpower each other with violent and tragic fury.

Here is that universal meaning I earlier sought in vain in those six characters. By going onstage on their own, and by struggling desperately against each other, as well as against the Director and the actors who do not understand them, they manage to discover the meaning within themselves. Unintentionally, unwittingly, in the confusion of their troubled souls, as each one defends the self against the accusations of the other, each expresses as his or her vivid passion and torment the passions and torments that for so many years constituted my own mental anguish: the deception of

3. In his essay *L'Umorismo,* Pirandello uses the word *umoristico* to describe the mixed feelings of laughter and sympathy, or comic and tragic modes, that a character may evoke. See Introduction above, p. xv–xvi.

mutual understanding hopelessly based on the empty abstraction of words; everyone's multiple personality, attributable to the range of possibilities that exist in each of us, and finally the inherent tragic conflict between life, which is continuously moving and changing, and the form it takes, which is fixed and immutable.

Two of these six characters especially, the Father and the Stepdaughter, speak of this atrocious, unbreakable rigidity of the form in which both see their essences expressed, forever immutable. For him this means punishment and for her revenge. They defend these essences against the thoughtless inconstancy of the actors, and they try to impose it on the vulgar Director who seeks to transform and adapt it to the so-called demands of the theater.

Not all six characters appear on the same level of formation, but this is not because they are divided into first- and second-class figures, or main and secondary characters. For their purposes, they are all fully formed. All six of them are at the same stage of artistic realization and all six on the same level of reality, which is the imaginary level of the play. The Father, the Stepdaughter and the Son are realized as mind, the Mother as nature, while the Boy, who watches, gesturing, along with the completely inert Little Girl, are simply present. This creates a new sort of perspective. Without being aware of it, I had felt the need to make some of them appear to be more (artistically) realized, others less so and others barely sketched in as elements to be told or shown. The most alive, the most fully created, are the Father and the Stepdaughter, who naturally stand out more, dragging behind them the dead weight of the others. These are the reluctant Son and the Mother, a passive victim between those two young children who have almost no substance except in appearance and who have to be led by the hand.

And that is indeed how they should appear — at the stage of creation achieved in the author's imagination at the precise moment when he wanted to send them off. In retrospect, after intuiting this necessity and finding the way to resolve it from a different angle, it all seems miraculous. The truth is that the play was conceived in a spark of the imagination when all the elements of the mind converged in divine agreement. No human brain working away calmly and patiently could ever have succeeded in penetrating and satisfying all that the form demands. Therefore, the ideas I will express here in an attempt to clarify the play's meaning should not be seen as something that I intended before I started writing the play or as a defense of it. Rather, they are discoveries that I was able to make later, with my mind at rest.

I wanted to portray six characters searching for an author. They do not succeed in creating a drama precisely because the author they are searching for is absent. What is staged instead is the comedy of their vain attempt, with all its tragic content, based on the rejection of six characters.

But is it possible simultaneously to portray and reject a character? Obviously, in order to portray a character, one must first welcome it into one's imagination and thus give it expression. And that is what I did. I accepted and created those six characters. However, I accepted and created them as rejected, in search of another author.

I must now make clear what I rejected: not them, but their drama, which doubtlessly interests them more than anything else, but it did not interest me, for the reasons already mentioned. And, for a character, what is one's own drama? Every being created by the artistic imagination, in order to exist, must have his or her drama, a drama in which that being is a character. The drama is the character's raison d'être, necessary for its existence.

Thus I accepted the existence of those six while rejecting their raison d'être. I took the being, substituting a more complex function for its original function. This is a terrible and desperate situation especially for the Father and the Stepdaughter, who have more desire to live and are more conscious of being characters than the others. In sum, they absolutely require a drama; but their own drama, the only one that they can imagine, but which they see as being rejected. This is an impossible situation, a question of life or death, from which they want to escape at any cost. It is true that I have given them another reason to exist — another function — which is precisely that impossible situation: the drama of being both in search of an author and rejected by him. However, they are unable even to suspect that this might constitute their raison d'être, that in fact it has become, for these characters who already had their own lives, the true, necessary and sufficient reason for their existence. Even if told this, they would not believe it, because it is not possible to believe that the only justification for our lives lies in a torment that appears unjust and inexplicable to us.

For this reason I cannot imagine why I have been criticized on the grounds that the Father's character is not what it should be, because he stepped out of his nature and position as a character, from time to time invading and usurping the author's role. I, who understand those who don't understand me, see clearly that this criticism stems from the fact that the character expresses as his own a mental anguish that is recognizably mine. But this is perfectly natural and means absolutely nothing. This mental anguish in the character of the Father is rooted in causes and experienced for reasons that have nothing to do with the drama of my own personal experience. That consideration in itself would demonstrate the criticism's inconsistency, but I want to make it clear that my own personal mental anguish is something I can legitimately reflect in a character, as long as it is organic and natural to him.

My mental activity as it is realized in this work — meaning the activity that succeeds in creating a drama out of the six characters in search of an author — is something quite different. If the Father were a participant in this activity, if he were competing in the creation of the drama of being those characters without an author, then and only then would it be justifiable to say that he is sometimes the author himself, and therefore is not what he should be. But the Father suffers from being a "character in search of an author" rather than from being a creator of characters. He endures his situation as an inexplicable fatality against which he tries with all his might to rebel and which he tries to remedy. He is therefore precisely a "character in search of an author" and nothing more, even if he expresses my mental anguish as his own. If he participated in the author's activity, that fatality would be easily explained; that is, he would feel that he was accepted into the womb of the poet's imagination, despite being a rejected character. He would no longer have any reason to suffer the despair of not finding someone to affirm and create his life as a character. I mean that he would willingly accept the raison d'être assigned to him by the author and would renounce his own with no regrets, sending away the Director and the actors instead of seeing them as his only recourse.

There is one character, the Mother, who doesn't care at all about being given life. She has not the slightest doubt that she is already alive, nor did it ever occur to her to wonder how and why, in what way, she is alive. In other words, she is not aware of being a character in that she is never, not even for a moment, detached from her role. She doesn't know that she has a "role."

This turns out to be perfectly natural for her. Actually, her role as Mother does not in itself, in its naturalness, include mental activity, and she does not live as mind. She lives in an unending stream of feeling, so that she cannot become conscious of her life, which is to say of her *being* as a character. In spite of all this, she too, in her own way and for her own reasons, is searching for an author. At a certain point, she seems to be happy to be taken to the Director. Perhaps because she also hopes to *be given life* by him? No. It is because she hopes that the Director will let her play a scene with the Son, a scene into which she would pour much of her own life, but a scene that does not exist, that has never taken place nor could ever take place. She is to such an extent unaware of being a character, of having a life that is completely fixed and determined, moment by moment, in every gesture and every word.

She appears onstage with the other characters, but without understanding what they are having her do. Evidently, she imagines that the craving for life constantly assailing her husband and daughter — and the reason why she too finds herself on a stage — is nothing but one of the usual incomprehensible eccentricities of that man who is both tormented and tormenter and — worst of all — another rebellion from her, that poor wayward girl. The Mother is completely passive. The events of her life and what they mean to her, her character itself, are all determined by the others. Only once, because her maternal instinct rose up and rebelled, did she contradict anyone. That was to make it clear that she did not at all want to abandon either her son or her husband, because her son was taken away from her and her husband forced her to abandon him. But she is simply correcting facts: she knows nothing and she explains nothing. In a word, she is Nature, Nature fixed in the figure of a mother.

This character gave me a new kind of satisfaction, which I will not try to hide. Almost all my critics, instead of defining her with their usual word, "inhuman," which seems to be the peculiar and incorrigible characteristic of all my characters without exception, were kind enough to note "with great pleasure" that, finally, a *most human* figure had emerged from my imagination. I explain their praise in this way: my poor Mother is completely bound to a Mother's natural attitude, with no possibility of free mental activity. In other words, she is little more than a lump of flesh entirely devoted to the functions of giving birth to, nursing, caring for and loving her offspring, with no need to use her brain. Therefore, she is the epitome of the true and perfect human type. This must mean that nothing seems more superfluous in a human organism than the mind.

But the critics expected to dismiss the Mother with their praise, without taking the trouble to penetrate the poetic significance of this character in the play. Of course, she's a most human figure, since she's devoid of a mind, unaware of being what she is or uninterested in explaining it to herself. But the fact that she doesn't know she's a character doesn't prevent her from being one. That is her drama in my play. The clearest expression of this situation comes out in her cry to the Director when he points out that everything has already happened and therefore she has no reason to be weeping at this point. "No, it's happening now. It happens all the time! My suffering is not over, sir! I am alive and present, always, in every moment of my suffering. It always renews itself. It's always alive and present." She therefore *feels* this, without being conscious of it, as something inexplicable, but she feels it with such terrible force that she doesn't even think that it can be explained, either to herself or to the others. She simply feels it. She feels it as pain, and it is this immediate pain that cries out. Thus she reflects the inflexibility of life in a form, which, in a different manner, torments the Father and the Stepdaughter. With them it is mind; with her, nature. The mind rebels against the inflexibility of form and, insofar as possible, tries to take advantage of it. Nature, unless the senses rebel, weeps over it.

The inherent conflict between the movement of life and the inflexibility of form is the inexorable condition not only of the spiritual order but also of the natural one. Life, which has become rigid, in order to exist in our bodily form, kills that form little by little. The lament of that rigid nature is expressed in the irreparable, continuous aging of our bodies. The Mother's lament is in the same way passive and perpetual. Displayed in three faces, given meaning in three different and simultaneous dramas, this struggle between life and form finds its fullest expression in the play. Moreover, the Mother also expresses in her cry to the Director the particular value of artistic form — a form that does not congeal and that does not kill life and that life does not consume. If the Father and the Stepdaughter replayed their scene a hundred thousand times continuously, at the exact moment when the life of the work of art is to be expressed in the Mother's cry, that cry of hers would resound, unchanged and unchangeable in its form. It would resound not as a mechanical repetition determined by external forces, but on the contrary, alive and as if new each time, born all of a sudden but forever embalmed alive in its incorruptible form. Thus every time we open the book, we will find the living Francesca confessing her sweet sin to Dante, and if we read that passage a hundred thousand times in succession, Francesca will speak her words again, never repeating them mechanically, but as if for the first time, with such vivid and spontaneous passion that each time Dante will faint.[4] Everything that lives, by virtue of being alive, has a form, and for that very reason must die. The work of art, on the other hand, lives forever, precisely because it is form.

The birth of a character from the human imagination, a birth that is a step across the threshold between nothingness and eternity, can even happen suddenly, when spurred by necessity. In a fictional drama, it is enough to have a character do or say something necessary. The character is born, exactly as he or she should be. Thus, Madame Pace is born among the six characters. This seems to be a miracle, or rather a trick, realistically portrayed on the stage. But it is no trick. The birth is real. The new character is alive not because she was previously alive but because of the kind of character she is — she is "obliged" to be born, so to speak. For this reason, there is a rupture, a sudden change in the scene's level of reality. A character can be born in such a way only in the imagination of the poet, certainly not on the boards of a stage. Without anyone noticing, I suddenly changed the scene. At that moment I pulled it back into my imagination without taking it away from the gaze of the audience. That is to say, in place of the stage, I showed them my imagination in the act of creating in the form of that same stage. The sudden and uncontrollable transformation of an appearance from one level of reality to another is a miracle on par with those accomplished by the saint who makes his statue move. At that moment, the statue is certainly no longer made of either wood or stone, but it is not an arbitrary miracle. That stage, since it receives the imagined reality of the six characters, does not exist in itself as a fixed and immobile given, just as nothing in this play exists as given and preconceived. Everything there is in process, in

4. The reference is to the Paolo and Francesca episode in Canto V of Dante's *Inferno.*

motion, tentative and unexpected. Even the level of reality of the place where this formless life, longing to find its form, changes and changes again, thus succeeds in changing organically. When I thought of having Madame Pace born there on that stage, I felt that I could do it, and I did it. Had I realized that this birth was silently and almost imperceptibly undermining and reshaping the scene's level of reality, I certainly wouldn't have done it. I would have been appalled by its obvious lack of logic, and I would have destroyed the beauty of my work. My inspiration saved me from doing this because, as opposed to false logic, that birth from the imagination is sustained by real necessity in mysterious organic correlation with the entire life of the work.

Now I smile at anyone who tells me that my play is not as good as it could be because it is not well-composed but chaotic, or because it is overly romantic. I can understand this observation. Since the drama in which the six characters are involved appears to be tumultuous and disorderly, there is no logical development or connection among the events. This is certainly true. Even if I had gone out and searched for it with a lantern, I would not have been able to find a more disorderly, strange, arbitrary and complicated, that is to say "romantic," way of presenting "the drama in which the six characters are involved." True enough, but I didn't write that drama. I wrote a different one — I'm not going to repeat what it is — in which, among all the good characteristics, which can be found according to inclination, there is actually a subtle satire on romantic methods. My six characters passionately strive to outdo themselves in their roles in one drama while I am presenting them as characters in another — something they neither know about nor suspect. Thus their passionate excitement, characteristically romantic, is framed "humoristically,"[5] stuck in a void. And the characters' drama, presented not as it would have taken shape in my imagination had it been accepted there, but rather as a drama that I rejected, could only exist in my work as a situation-in-progress. It could not develop except by allusions, tumultuously and in a disorderly fashion, with violent disruptions, chaotically, continuously interrupted, sidetracked, contradicted, to the point of being denied by one of its characters and not even experienced by two of them.

5. See above footnote 3, p. 20.

Indeed there is one character — the one that denies the drama that makes him a character, the Son — that derives all his substance and value not from being a character in the play-to-be-made, in which he barely appears, but in the play that I made of it. In other words, he is the only one who lives entirely as a "character in search of an author," to such a degree that the author he is searching for is not a dramatic author. This, too, could not be otherwise: just as the character's attitude is organic in my conception, so it is logical that in this situation this attitude should cause greater confusion and disorder and become another element of romantic contrast.

But it was precisely this organic and natural chaos that I had to portray, and portraying chaos does not at all mean portraying chaotically, that is, romantically. And the fact is, my portrayal is anything but confused. On the contrary, it is quite clear, simple and orderly. Audiences all over the world have understood the clarity of the plot and characters as well as the imaginary, realistic, dramatic and comic levels of the work. For those with more penetrating eyes, the unusual meanings within the play emerge.

How confused are human languages if there are words in them to express such criticisms. The confusion is as great as the deep law of order is perfect. This law, which I have obeyed in all respects, makes my work classical and typical and does not allow words to articulate the play's catastrophe. It is clear to everyone that life cannot be artificially created and that the drama of the six characters, lacking the authority of an author, cannot be staged by a director vulgar enough to worry about how the plot unfolds. The Son recounts the succession of events in the plot — a narrative lacking in meaning and that does not need a human voice. The catastrophe occurs brutally, uselessly, with the firing of a mechanical weapon on the stage, breaking up and dispersing the sterile attempt of the characters and the actors to make their play without the help of the poet.

Meanwhile, unbeknownst to them, and as though having watched their effort all along from afar, the poet has been waiting to create, with it and from it, his work.

Six Characters in Search of an Author: A Play to Be Made[1]

Characters in the Play to Be Made

The Father
The Mother
The Stepdaughter
The Son
The Young Boy (non-speaking)
The Little Girl (non-speaking)
Madame Pace *(evoked later)*

The Theater Company

The Director
The Lead Actress
The Lead Actor
The Supporting Actress
The Young Actress
The Young Actor
Other Actors and Actresses
The Stage Manager
The Prompter
The Prop Man
The Head Stagehand
The Director's Secretary
The Head Usher
Stagehands

Daytime, onstage in a theater

N.B. The play has neither acts nor scenes. The performance should be interrupted for the first time — without the curtain falling — when the Director *and the* Father *go offstage to put together the scenario*

1. Translated from *Sei personaggi in cerca d'autore: Commedia da fare,* in Alessandro d'Amico, ed., Luigi Pirandello, *Maschere Nude* (Milan: Mondadori, 2001), 2:668–758. Final (1937) edition, slightly revised from 1925 edition.

and the ACTORS *clear the stage. The second interruption should occur when the* HEAD STAGEHAND *mistakenly lowers the curtain.*

Upon entering the theater, the audience will find the curtain raised and the stage as it is during the day, without wings or scenery, almost dark and empty. From the start they should have the impression that this show has not been rehearsed.

Two stairways, one on the right and one on the left, connect the stage with the auditorium. Onstage, the top has been taken off the prompter's box and lies next to it. Opposite, downstage, is the DIRECTOR'S *table and his armchair with its back toward the audience. Two other little tables, one larger than the other, with several chairs around them, are placed downstage so as to be ready, if needed, for the rehearsal. More chairs are scattered around left and right for the* ACTORS. *Upstage, a piano, off to one side, is practically hidden.*

Once the house lights are off, the STAGEHAND, *wearing dark blue overalls, with a tool kit hanging from his belt, enters from the stage door. He goes to get some boards from a corner upstage, brings them downstage and kneels to drive nails into them. As the hammer strikes, the* STAGE MANAGER *rushes in from the door that leads to the dressing rooms.*

STAGE MANAGER Oh! What are you doing?

HEAD STAGEHAND What do you think I'm doing? I'm hammering nails.

STAGE MANGER Now? *(He looks at his watch.)* It's already ten thirty. The director's going to be here any minute for the rehearsal.

HEAD STAGEHAND Yeah, but I've got to have time to do my work, too.

STAGE MANAGER You'll have time. But not now.

HEAD STAGEHAND Then when?

STAGE MANAGER When it's not rehearsal time. Now get going, clear away your stuff, and let me set the stage for the second act of *The Rules of the Game.*

The HEAD STAGEHAND, *huffing and puffing, picks up the boards and exits. In the meantime, the company* ACTORS, *men and women, begin to enter through the stage door. They come onstage first one by one, then two by two or more. Finally, there are nine or ten, as many as are supposed to be participating in the rehearsal of Pirandello's play* The Rules of the Game, *scheduled for the day. As they enter, they greet the* STAGE MANAGER *and each other. Some go to their dressing rooms. The others — including the* PROMPTER, *who has the play script rolled up under his arm — remain onstage waiting for the* DIRECTOR *to begin the rehearsal. Seated in groups or standing, they chat among themselves. One of them might light a cigarette; one might complain about her assigned role; one might read aloud to his colleagues a news item from a theater journal. Both the male and female* ACTORS *should wear light and brightly-colored costumes, and this first improvised scene should be played in a natural and lively manner. At a certain point, one of the* ACTORS *could sit down at the piano and play a dance tune, and the youngest members of the troupe might start dancing.*

STAGE MANAGER *(clapping his hands to call them to order)* That's enough. Stop it! Here's the Director!

The music and dancing stop all of a sudden. The ACTORS *turn around to look toward the audience as the* DIRECTOR *enters from the rear door. Wearing a top hat, with a walking stick under his arm and a fat cigar in his mouth, he walks down an aisle between the seats, acknowledges the* ACTORS' *greetings, and climbs up one of the two stairways to the stage.* DIRECTOR'S SECRETARY *gives him the mail: newspapers and a script in a wrapper.*

DIRECTOR Any letters?

DIRECTOR'S SECRETARY None. This is all the mail.

DIRECTOR *(handing him the script)* Take this to my office. *(then looking around and turning toward the* STAGE MANAGER*)* We can't even see each other here. Please tell them to turn up the lights.

STAGE MANAGER Right away.

He goes off to give the order. A little later, the whole right side of the stage, where the ACTORS *are, is fully illuminated with a brilliant white light. In the meantime, the* PROMPTER *takes his place in his box, turns on his flashlight and spreads the script in front of him.*

DIRECTOR *(clapping his hands)* Come, come, let's get started! *(to the* STAGE MANAGER*)* Is someone missing?

STAGE MANAGER The leading lady.

DIRECTOR As usual! *(looking at his watch)* We're already ten minutes late. Mark her down for it, will you? Maybe she'll learn to get to rehearsals on time. *(Before he finishes his reprimand, the LEAD ACTRESS's voice is heard from the back of the auditorium.)*

LEAD ACTRESS No, no, please! Here I am! Here I am! *(She is dressed all in white, with an outrageous hat on her head and a cute little dog in her arms. She runs down the aisle and rushes up one of the stairways.)*

DIRECTOR It seems you've taken a vow to always make us wait.

LEAD ACTRESS My apologies. I looked everywhere for a taxi so I could get here on time! But I see you haven't yet begun. And I don't go onstage right away. *(calling the STAGE MANAGER by name and handing him the little dog)* Please put him in my dressing room.

DIRECTOR *(muttering)* And the doggie as well! As if there weren't enough dogs around here. *(He claps his hands again and turns to the PROMPTER.)* OK, let's get going. Act 2 of *The Rules of the Game*. *(sitting down in his armchair)* Who's onstage?

The ACTORS and ACTRESSES clear out from the front of the stage and go to sit on one side, except for the three who are to begin the rehearsal and the LEAD ACTRESS, who, paying no attention to the DIRECTOR's question, sits down at one of the two tables.

DIRECTOR *(to the LEAD ACTRESS)* So you're in this scene?

LEAD ACTRESS I? No, sir.

DIRECTOR *(annoyed)* Then for the love of God get off the stage! *(The LEAD ACTRESS rises and goes to sit next to the other ACTORS who have already moved aside.)*

DIRECTOR *(to the PROMPTER)* Let's get going!

PROMPTER *(reading from the script)* "In Leone Gala's house. A strange dining room/study."

DIRECTOR *(turning toward the STAGE MANAGER)* We'll use the red room set.

STAGE MANAGER *(writing on a piece of paper)* Ok, the red one.

PROMPTER *(continuing to read from the script)* "Dining table set and desk covered with books and papers. Shelves full of books.

Glass-fronted cabinets filled with expensive tableware. Exit downstage leading to Leone's bedroom. Side exit to the left leading to the kitchen. Main exit to the right."

DIRECTOR *(rising and pointing)* Now pay close attention. Main exit, over there. Kitchen, this way. *(addressing the actor who will play the part of Socrates)* You will enter and exit this way. *(to the STAGE MANAGER)* You'll need to put up an inner door and curtains at the back. *(He returns to his seat.)*

STAGE MANAGER *(taking notes)* OK.

PROMPTER *(reading as before)* Scene 1. Leone Gala, Guido Venanzi, Filippo, known as Socrates." *(to the DIRECTOR)* Do I have to read the stage directions too?

DIRECTOR Yes, of course! I've told you so a hundred times!

PROMPTER *(reading as before)* "As the curtain rises, Leone Gala, wearing a chef's hat and apron, is concentrating on beating an egg in a bowl with a wooden spoon. Filippo, also dressed as a cook, is beating another egg. Guido Venanzi listens, seated."

LEAD ACTOR *(to the DIRECTOR)* Excuse me, do I really have to put on a chef's hat?

DIRECTOR *(irritated by the remark)* What do you think? It's written right there! *(He points to the script.)*

LEAD ACTOR I'm sorry, but that's ridiculous.

DIRECTOR *(jumping up, furious)* "Ridiculous! Ridiculous!" What am I supposed to do when we're not getting any more good French plays, and we're reduced to putting on incomprehensible plays by Pirandello, deliberately written to grate on actors, critics and audiences? *(The ACTORS laugh. The DIRECTOR then gets up, goes to the lead actor, and screams)* Yes, sir, the chef's hat! And beat those eggs! Do you think you are doing nothing else but beating eggs? Ha! You have to represent the shells of those eggs. *(The ACTORS go back to laughing and begin to make sarcastic comments to one another.)* Quiet! And listen while I explain! *(addressing the LEAD ACTOR again)* Yes, sir, the shell. It's supposed to signify the empty form of reason, unfilled by instinct, which is blind! You are reason. Your wife is instinct. Those are the rules of the game. You have to play according to them, and when you act the role assigned to you, you deliberately become your own puppet. Get it?

LEAD ACTOR *(spreading out his arms)* No way!

DIRECTOR *(returning to his place)* I don't either. Let's get on with it; I think you'll like the ending. *(confidentially)* Please keep yourself turned three-quarters toward the audience. Otherwise, between the obscurity of the dialogue and you not making yourself heard, we're done for! *(clapping his hands again)* Listen up! Let's begin!

PROMPTER Excuse me, sir. Can I put the top on my box? There's a draft.

DIRECTOR Of course, go ahead, go ahead.

The HEAD USHER, wearing a gold-braided cap, has entered the theater. Walking down the aisle between the orchestra seats, he approaches the stage to tell the DIRECTOR about the arrival of SIX CHARACTERS who have also entered the theater, following him at a certain distance and looking around, appearing dazed and perplexed.

Whoever attempts to stage this play must use every means at hand to create an effect showing that these SIX CHARACTERS are not to be confused with the COMPANY ACTORS. Positioning the two groups onstage, as indicated in the stage directions, will no doubt help, as will different colors of lighting achieved by appropriate reflectors. But the most effective and suitable way, recommended here, is the use of specially-made masks for the CHARACTERS. These masks should be constructed of material that will not soften from sweat yet not be too heavy for the ACTORS. They should be cut so as to leave the eyes, nostrils and mouth free. This will also bring out the play's deeper meaning. The CHARACTERS should not appear to be ghosts, but rather created realities, changeless constructions of the imagination: thus both more real and more consistent than the shifting naturalness of the ACTORS. The masks will help to give the impression of figures created by art, each one immutably fixed in the expression of his or her most basic emotion. For the FATHER, it is remorse; for the STEPDAUGHTER, revenge; for the SON, contempt; for the MOTHER, sorrow. Her mask should have wax tears fixed on the shadows under the eye holes and along the cheeks, as in the sculpted and painted images of the Mater dolorosa one sees in churches. Their costumes should also be made of special fabric and specially designed — nothing extravagant — but with stiff folds, almost statuesque, making it obvious that they weren't made of the kind of fabric sold anywhere in the city or cut and sewn by just any seamstress.

The FATHER is in his fifties, not bald, but with thinning reddish hair and thick whiskers around his mouth, which still appears young and is often opened in an uncertain and meaningless smile. He is pale with a broad forehead and extremely bright and piercing, oval, blue eyes. He wears light pants and a dark jacket. Sometimes he seems sweet and gentle, and at other times he erupts harshly and bitterly. The MOTHER appears to be terrified, as if crushed by an unbearable weight of shame and humiliation. Her face is covered by a thick widow's veil; she is humbly dressed in black. When she lifts the veil, her face does not show suffering, but seems to be made of wax, and she always keeps her eyes cast down.

The STEPDAUGHTER, eighteen, is insolent, almost brazen. She is very beautiful and also dressed in mourning, but with showy elegance. She manifests contempt for her fearful, afflicted and almost lost-looking younger brother, a miserable YOUNG BOY of fourteen, also dressed in black. On the other hand, she displays a lively tenderness for her little sister, a four-year-old LITTLE GIRL dressed in white with a black silk sash around her waist. The SON, twenty-two, is tall, rigid with repressed scorn for his FATHER and sullen indifference towards his MOTHER. He is wearing a purple overcoat with a long green scarf wound around his neck.

HEAD USHER *(cap in hand, to the DIRECTOR)* Excuse me, sir.

DIRECTOR *(rudely, angrily)* What now?

HEAD USHER *(timidly)* Some people are here asking for you. *(Astonished, the DIRECTOR and the ACTORS turn to look down from the stage into the auditorium.)*

DIRECTOR *(furious again)* I'm rehearsing! You know very well that no one's allowed in here during rehearsals! *(looking toward the back of the auditorium)* Who are you people? What do you want?

FATHER *(moving forward, followed by the others, to one of the two staircases)* We are here in search of an author.

DIRECTOR *(at once amazed and angry)* An author? What author?

FATHER Any author, sir.

DIRECTOR Well, there are no authors here. We're not rehearsing any new plays.

STEPDAUGHTER *(excitedly running up the staircase)* So much the better, so much the better then, sir. *We* can be your new play.

SOME ACTORS *(amid the loud comments and laughter of the others)* Just listen to that!

FATHER *(following the STEPDAUGHTER onto the stage)* Yes, but there's no author here? *(to the DIRECTOR)* Unless you would like to be....

The YOUNG BOY and the MOTHER, holding the LITTLE GIRL by the hand, walk up the first steps of the stairway and stand there waiting. The SON, brooding, remains below.

DIRECTOR Is this some sort of joke?

FATHER No, not at all, what are you saying, sir? Just the opposite: we are bringing you a painful drama.

STEPDAUGHTER And we could make your fortune!

DIRECTOR Please do me a favor and leave. We don't have time to waste with crazy people.

FATHER *(hurt, but sweet and gentle)* Oh, sir, you know that life is full of infinite absurdities which — brazenly — don't even need to seem true, because they are true.

DIRECTOR What the hell are you talking about?

FATHER I'm saying that it could actually be considered madness to attempt to do the opposite: to create things in order to make them seem true. But allow me to point out that if this is madness, it is also the only reason for your profession and your actors' profession. *(The ACTORS make indignant gestures.)*

DIRECTOR *(standing and staring him down)* So that's what you think? Our profession is for the mad?

FATHER Well, to make what is not true seem true, not out of need, sir, but for fun.... Isn't it your job to give imaginary characters a life on the stage?

DIRECTOR *(immediately, speaking for his ACTORS who are growing more and more indignant)* My dear sir, I'll have you know that the actor's profession is a most noble one! Nowadays the new playwrights give us nothing but silly scripts and puppets instead of real people to put on stage. But you should be aware that we are proud of having given life — here, on these boards — to immortal works! *(Contented, the ACTORS applaud their DIRECTOR approvingly.)*

FATHER *(interrupting and taking up the argument)* That's right! Exactly! To living beings, more alive than those who breathe and wear clothes! Not as real, perhaps, but more true! We are of the very same opinion! *(The ACTORS look at each other in amazement.)*

DIRECTOR What? Before, you said...

FATHER No, sir, I'm sorry. I said that to you when you were yelling at us that you didn't have time to waste with crazy people. No one knows better than you that Nature uses human imagination to pursue her creative work on a higher plane.

DIRECTOR OK, fine. But where are you going with this?

FATHER Nowhere, sir. I want to demonstrate to you that one can be born in many ways, in many forms: as a tree or a stone, water or a butterfly...or a woman. And that one can also be born as a character!

DIRECTOR *(with feigned and ironic surprise)* And you, like these people with you, were born a character?

FATHER Exactly, sir. And alive, just as you see us. *(The DIRECTOR and the ACTORS break out in laughter, as if having heard a joke.)*

FATHER *(hurt)* I'm sorry that you're laughing like that because, as I said, we bear within us a painful drama, as you can all tell from this woman veiled in black.

As he says this, he extends his hand to the MOTHER to help her walk up the last few stairs and, continuing to hold her by the hand, he takes her, in a tragically solemn manner, to the opposite side of the stage, which is suddenly illuminated with an otherworldly light. The LITTLE GIRL and the YOUNG BOY follow the MOTHER. Then the SON, keeping himself apart from the group, moves upstage. The STEPDAUGHTER, who also keeps her distance, goes downstage and leans on the proscenium arch. The ACTORS, first amazed and then enthused by this development, applaud as though having just seen a performance.

DIRECTOR *(at first dumfounded, then scornful)* Come on, now! Silence! *(then, turning toward the CHARACTERS)* Away with you! Get out of here! *(to the STAGE MANAGER)* For God's sake, get them out of here!

STAGE MANAGER *(moving forward, but then stopping, as if restrained by an eerie sense of anguish)* Out! Out!

FATHER *(to the DIRECTOR)* No, please, you see, we...

DIRECTOR *(shouting)* Now look here, we have work to do!

LEAD ACTOR It's not okay to play tricks like this on us.

FATHER *(determined, moving forward)* I'm astounded by your disbelief! Aren't you ladies and gentlemen used to seeing characters created by an author make their live appearance here on stage, confronting each other? Maybe it's because there's no script that contains us in there *(points to the Prompter's box).*

STEPDAUGHTER *(sidling up to the DIRECTOR, smiling, alluringly)* Believe me, sir, we really are six very interesting characters. But abandoned, lost.

FATHER *(swerving past her)* Yes, exactly, lost and abandoned! *(to the DIRECTOR)* In the sense, you see, that the author who created us wouldn't — or couldn't — put us into the world of art. And that, sir, was a real crime, because whoever has the good fortune to be born as a live character can even laugh at death. He will never die! The man will die, the writer, the instrument of creation: the creation will never die! And in order to live forever, a character doesn't even need to be a genius or to work wonders. Who was Sancho Panza? Who was Don Abbondio?[2] And yet they have eternal life because as living embryos they had the good fortune to find a fertile womb, an imagination that was able to nurture them and help them grow — to make them live for eternity.

DIRECTOR That's all well and good. But what do you want here?

FATHER We want to live!

DIRECTOR *(ironically)* For eternity?

FATHER No, Sir, but at least for a moment, in all of you.

AN ACTOR Oh my God!

LEAD ACTRESS They want to live in us!

YOUNG ACTOR *(indicating the STEPDAUGHTER)* OK with me, if I can have that one.

---

2. The former is a character is Cervantes' Don Quixote; the latter a character in Alessandro Manzoni's *I promessi sposi (The Betrothed),* a novel published in final form in 1842 and well-known to Italians. A character well-known to English speakers — Falstaff, for example — could be substituted.

FATHER Now, look here. The play is yet to be made. *(to the DIRECTOR)* But if you and your actors are willing, we can orchestrate it right now among us!

DIRECTOR *(annoyed)* What do you mean, "orchestrate"? We're not working with orchestras here! Here we put on dramas and comedies!

FATHER That's just fine! That's exactly why we came to you.

DIRECTOR And where's the script?

FATHER It's in us, sir. *(The ACTORS laugh.)* The drama is in us. We are the drama, and we are anxious to perform it just as our inner passions guide us.

STEPDAUGHTER *(playfully, with treacherous charm loaded with impudence)* *My* passion, if you only knew, Sir! *My* passion…for him! *(She points to the FATHER, almost embracing him, but then bursts into strident laughter.)*

FATHER *(in a fit of anger)* Be quiet! And I beg you not to laugh like that!

STEPDAUGHTER No? Well then, if I have everyone's permission, just watch me — though I lost my father only two months ago — sing and dance! *(Maliciously, she begins to sing the refrain of "Beware of Chou-Chin-Chow" composed by Dave Stamper, lyrics by Gene Buck, arranged as a foxtrot or a slow one-step by Francis Salabert, with French lyrics by Lucien Boyer, doing a dance step to it.[3])*

Les chinois sont un people malin,
De Shangaï à Pékin,
Ils ont mis des écriteaux partout:
Prenez garde à Tchou-Tchin-Tchou!

While she is dancing and singing, the ACTORS, notably the young ones, as if drawn by a strange charm, move towards her, raising their hands as though to grab her. She runs from them. When the ACTORS begin to applaud and the DIRECTOR disapproves, she appears withdrawn and distant.

ACTORS AND ACTRESSES *(laughing and applauding)* Brava! Well done! Great!

3. See the Appendix with the music and both the English and French lyrics.

DIRECTOR *(angry)* Quiet! Where do you think you are, in a music hall? *(taking the FATHER aside, somewhat worried)* Tell me, is she crazy?

FATHER No, not crazy. It's worse!

STEPDAUGHTER *(rushing to the DIRECTOR)* Worse! Worse! That's right, worse! Listen, please, let us perform our drama right away. Because you'll see that at a certain point, I — when my little angel here *(she takes the hand of the LITTLE GIRL, who is standing next to the MOTHER, and leads her to the DIRECTOR)* — don't you see how pretty she is? *(She takes the LITTLE GIRL in her arms and kisses her.)* Darling! darling! *(She puts her down and adds, moved and almost involuntarily)* Well, when God all of a sudden takes this little angel away from her poor mother, and this imbecile here *(she pushes the YOUNG BOY forward, grabbing him rudely by the sleeve)* does the stupidest thing of all, like the fool that he is *(she shoves him back toward the MOTHER),* then you'll see me fly away! Yes, sir! Fly away, fly away! And I can't wait, believe me, I can't wait. Because after all the intimate things that transpired between me and him *(she gestures toward the FATHER with a horrible wink),* I can't stand to be with them any longer, watching our mother suffer because of that jerk over there *(she indicates the SON)*. Look at him, look at him! He's icy-cold. He doesn't give a damn, because *he's* the legitimate son! Full of scorn for me, for that boy *(indicates the YOUNG BOY),* for that dear little girl, because we're bastards — get it? — bastards! *(She goes to the MOTHER and hugs her.)* And he doesn't want to recognize this poor mother, the common mother of all of us, her as *his* mother. Instead he snubs her and sees her as nothing but the mother of us three bastards. Vile! *(She speaks quickly, excitedly. After raising her voice on the word "bastards," when she gets to the last word, "vile," she pronounces it softly, almost spitting it out.)*

MOTHER *(to the DIRECTOR, with great anguish)* I beg you, sir, for the sake of these two little children.... *(She begins to faint and stumbles.)* Oh, God....

FATHER *(rushing over to hold her up with almost all the ACTORS, who show amazement and concern)* For heaven's sake, please, a chair, a chair for this poor widow.

ACTORS *(gathering around her)* So it's true? She's really fainting?

DIRECTOR Bring a chair here, at once!

One of the ACTORS brings a chair. The others continue to gather around the MOTHER, showing their concern. The MOTHER, seated, tries to prevent the FATHER from lifting the veil that hides her face.

FATHER Look at her, sir. Just look at her.

MOTHER Please, no. For God's sake, stop it!

FATHER Let them see you. *(He lifts her veil.)*

MOTHER *(standing up and desperately covering her face with her hands)* Oh, sir, I beg you. Don't let this man carry out his plan. It is horrible for me!

DIRECTOR *(overcome, baffled)* I don't understand anything anymore. Where are we? What's all this about? *(to the FATHER)* Is this lady your wife?

FATHER *(immediately)* Yes, of course, my wife.

DIRECTOR So then, how come she's a widow, if you're alive? *(The Actors release all of their anxiety and confusion in a roar of laughter.)*

FATHER *(hurt, with bitter resentment)* Don't laugh! Don't laugh like that. Have pity! This is exactly the stuff of her drama, sir. She had another man. Another man, who should be here!

MOTHER *(crying out)* No! No!

STEPDAUGHTER Lucky for him, he died — two months ago, as I told you. We're still in mourning for him, as you can see.

FATHER But the reason he's not here, you see, is not because he's dead. He's not here because — look at her, sir, and you'll understand right away! Her drama could not be made of her love for two men — she's incapable of feeling anything for them except maybe a little gratitude (not toward me, toward the other man!*)*. She's not a woman; she's a mother! And her drama — which is powerful, sir, powerful — resides entirely in these four children fathered by the two different men that she had.

MOTHER *I* had *them*! You have the gall to say that I was the one who "had" them, as if I had wanted them? *He* was the one, sir! He was the one who gave me to the other man. He forced me! He made me. He made me run away with that man!

STEPDAUGHTER *(brusquely, outraged)* It's not true!

MOTHER *(shocked)* What do you mean it's not true?

STEPDAUGHTER It's not true! It's not true!

MOTHER And what can you possibly know about it?

STEPDAUGHTER It's not true! *(to the DIRECTOR)* Don't believe it! Do you know why she's saying that? Because of *him (she points to the SON).* She's saying it for his sake. Because she's tearing herself apart. She's killing herself, all because of his indifference to her. So she wants to make him believe that, if she abandoned him when he was two years old, it was because he *(she points to the FATHER)* forced her into it.

MOTHER He *did* force me, as God is my witness. He forced me! *(to the DIRECTOR)* Just ask him *(she points at her HUSBAND)* if it's not true! Make him say so!... She *(she points at her DAUGHTER)* can't possibly know anything about it.

STEPDAUGHTER Well, I know that as long as my father lived, you were happy and at peace. Deny it, if you can!

MOTHER I don't deny it, no...

STEPDAUGHTER He was always full of love and care for you! *(to the YOUNG BOY, angrily)* Isn't that true? Say so! Why don't you speak up, you dummy?

MOTHER Please leave that poor boy alone! Why do you, my own daughter, want everyone to think that I'm ungrateful? I don't want to offend your father, not at all! I just wanted to say that it wasn't my fault and that I didn't leave my home and my son for my own pleasure!

FATHER It's true, sir. I was the one responsible.

LEAD ACTOR *(to his fellow ACTORS)* What a show!

LEAD ACTRESS They're the ones putting on the show for us!

YOUNG ACTOR For once, anyway!

DIRECTOR *(beginning to get really interested)* Listen! Let's listen to them! *(As he speaks this line, he goes down one of the staircases and stands in front of the stage, as if to get a spectator's view of the scene.)*

SON *(without moving from his place, coldly, quietly, ironically)* Yes, everyone listen now to the pseudo-philosopher. He'll tell you all about the "Demon of Experimentation."

FATHER You're a cynical imbecile, as I've told you a hundred times! *(speaking down to the DIRECTOR)* He ridicules me, sir, because of that phrase, which I use to justify myself.

SON *(disdainfully)* Phrases!

FATHER Phrases! Phrases! As if everyone, confronted with an inexplicable fact, with something horrible that tears us apart, didn't try to find peace in the same manner — in a word that doesn't mean anything but that gives us comfort!

STEPDAUGHTER Even — in fact, especially — when it comes to remorse!

FATHER Remorse? No, that's not true. I never freed myself from remorse with words alone.

STEPDAUGHTER Then with a little money as well. Yes, yes, a little money too. With the cash that he was about to pay me, ladies and gentlemen! *(gestures of horror on the part of the ACTORS)*

SON *(to his STEPSISTER with disdain)* That is vile!

STEPDAUGHTER Vile? There was the cash in a light blue envelope on the little mahogany table in the back room of Madame Pace's boutique. You know what I mean? One of those *Madames* who, under the pretense of selling coats and dresses, lure us poor girls from good families into their shops.

SON And she bought herself the right to tyrannize all of us, with that money that he was about to pay and that, luckily — listen closely — he had no reason to pay!

STEPDAUGHTER Oh, but we were just about to do it! *(She bursts out laughing.)*

MOTHER *(rising, in revulsion)* For shame, daughter, for shame!

STEPDAUGHTER *(brusquely)* Shame? This is my revenge! I'm trembling, sir. I'm dying to live that scene! The room...there's the window display of coats. There's the sofa bed, the mirror, a screen. And in front of the window is that little mahogany table with the light blue envelope containing the cash. I can see it! I could take it! But the gentlemen should turn away. I'm almost naked! I'm not blushing anymore, because he's the one blushing now! *(she points to the FATHER)* But I assure you that he was very pale, very pale, at that moment! *(to the DIRECTOR)* Believe me, sir!

DIRECTOR I'm completely lost!

FATHER Of course you are, when you're assaulted like that! Impose a little order, sir, and let me speak. Don't let this furious girl slander me without listening to my explanations!

STEPDAUGHTER Here on stage you can't narrate! You can't narrate!

FATHER I have no intention of narrating! I just want to explain to him....

STEPDAUGHTER Oh, right. In *your* way. *(At this point the DIRECTOR goes back on stage to restore order.)*

FATHER But here lies the source of all the trouble. In words! We all have within us a world of things — each one a private world of things. How can we possibly understand each other, sir, if I imbue the words I speak with the meaning and the value of things as they are inside me, while those who hear my words inevitably interpret them with their own meanings and values in the world they have inside themselves? We think we understand each other! We never understand each other! Look! All my pity, all my pity for this woman! *(he points to the MOTHER)* She understood as the fiercest sort of cruelty!

MOTHER But he threw me out!

FATHER There, do you hear her? Threw her out! It seemed to her that I threw her out!

MOTHER You know how to speak. I don't. But believe me, sir, after he married me — and who knows why...? I was a poor, humble woman....

FATHER But it was precisely because you were humble that I married you. That's what I loved in you, believing.... *(He interrupts himself when she shakes her head "no." He opens his arms in a desperate gesture, and seeing that it is impossible to make her understand him, he turns to the DIRECTOR.)* Don't you see? She says, "No!" It's frightening. Believe me, it's frightening, *(he hits himself on the forehead)* her deafness, her mental deafness! A heart, yes, she has a heart for her children. But she's deaf, brain-deaf, so deaf she can drive you to despair!

STEPDAUGHTER Right, right, but now make him tell everyone what good his intelligence has done us!

FATHER If we could only predict all the evil that comes from the good that we think we are doing!

(At this point, the LEAD ACTRESS, who has been seething from watching the LEAD ACTOR flirt with the STEPDAUGHTER, comes forward and addresses the DIRECTOR.)

LEAD ACTRESS Excuse me, but are we going to continue with the rehearsal?

DIRECTOR Of course! Of course! Just let me listen for a while!

YOUNG ACTOR It's a completely new case!

YOUNG ACTRESS So interesting!

LEAD ACTRESS To those who are interested! *(She throws a glance at the LEAD ACTOR.)*

DIRECTOR *(to the FATHER)* But you must explain yourself clearly. *(He sits down.)*

FATHER Yes, all right. You see, there was a poor man working for me. He was my secretary and very devoted. He and my wife got along together perfectly, without any hint of misconduct — understand this! He was kind and humble like her, both of them incapable of thinking, much less doing, anything wrong.

STEPDAUGHTER And so *he* thought it up for them — and did it!

FATHER That's not true! I was trying to do the right thing for them, and for myself as well, I admit! I had reached the point where I couldn't say a word to him or to her without both of them immediately exchanging a look of understanding. She would look him in the eye right away as if seeking advice on how to react to my words in order not to enrage me. This was enough, as you can see, to keep me in a state of constant rage and unbearable exasperation!

DIRECTOR Well then, why didn't you just fire that secretary of yours?

FATHER Of course! I sent him away! But then I had to watch that poor woman around the house like a lost soul, like a stray animal that you adopt out of charity.

MOTHER Ha! But…!

FATHER *(immediately turning toward her as if to anticipate what she will say)* Your son, right?

MOTHER First he took my son from my breast, sir!

FATHER But not out of cruelty! It was so he could grow up healthy and strong, in touch with the earth!

STEPDAUGHTER *(pointing at the SON, ironically)* As you can see!

FATHER *(immediately)* Ah, so that's my fault too, is it, if he turned out like this? In the country, I had given him to a wet-nurse, sir, a farm woman. My wife didn't seem strong enough to me, even though she was of humble birth. It was for the same reason that I married her. A silly idea, no doubt, but there it is. I've always had these damnable aspirations for a certain strong moral health! *(At this point the STEPDAUGHTER breaks out again in peals of laughter.)* Please make her stop! It's unbearable!

DIRECTOR Stop it! Let me listen, for the love of God! *(Once again she stops suddenly, in the midst of a laugh, becoming aloof and withdrawn upon hearing the DIRECTOR's rebuke. The DIRECTOR again leaves the stage to try to get an impression of the scene.)*

FATHER I could no longer see myself next to this woman. *(He gestures towards the MOTHER.)* It was not so much that she annoyed me — although her presence was stifling, truly stifling! — as because of the pity, the anguishing pity I felt for her.

MOTHER And he sent me away!

FATHER Yes, well provided for in every way, to that man, to free her from me!

MOTHER And to free himself!

FATHER Yes, sir, to free myself as well, I admit. And much evil came from it. But I did it in order to do good...and more for her than for me, I swear! *(He crosses his arms over his chest, then suddenly turns toward the MOTHER.)* I never lost sight of you, you know, never lost sight of you until he suddenly took you away to another town without my knowing it. Stupidly, he was bothered by my interest, my pure, pure interest — believe me, sir — without the slightest ulterior motive. Unbelievably, I became more and more interested in, and more affectionate toward, the little family she was raising. Even *she (pointing to the STEPDAUGHTER)* can attest to that!

STEPDAUGHTER I'll say! A little tiny girl, you know! With pigtails on my shoulders and bloomers longer than my skirt — just this high — I used to see him in front of the door of my school, as I was walking out. He was coming to watch me grow up....

FATHER This is treacherous. Shameful!

STEPDAUGHTER No, why?

FATHER Shameful! Shameful! *(Immediately turning to the DIRECTOR, trying to explain, in a state of agitation)* My house, sir, once she had left, *(points to the MOTHER)* seemed suddenly empty. She was my nightmare, but she had filled it! Alone, I found myself wandering through the rooms like a headless fly. That boy *(points to the SON)* — I don't know, maybe because he was raised elsewhere — didn't seem to belong to me anymore once he came back. With no mother between him and me, he grew up by himself, isolated. He had no emotional or intellectual relationship with me. And then — it may seem strange, sir, but it's true — I became at first curious about, and then bit by bit attracted to, her little family, which I had in a sense created. Thinking about it began to fill the emptiness. I needed, really needed, to believe that she was at peace, occupied with the simplest tasks in life, fortunate because she was away from my complicated spiritual torments. For evidence of this, I went to see that little girl as she was leaving school.

STEPDAUGHTER Right! He used to follow me on my way home, smiling, and when I reached my house he waved at me — like this! I would glare at him. I didn't know who he was! I told my mother. She must have understood right away that it was him. *(The MOTHER nods, "yes.")* At first, for several days, she wouldn't send me to school. When I went back, I saw him again at the school door — the buffoon — with a package in his hand wrapped in paper. He came up to me, petted me, unwrapped the package and took out a big, beautiful straw hat from Florence with a garland of young roses. For me!

DIRECTOR But all this is just storytelling, my friends.

SON *(disdainful)* Exactly. Literature! Literature!

FATHER Literature? No, sir. This is life! Passion!

DIRECTOR That may be so, but it can't be staged!

FATHER Of course. Because all this is just background. I'm not saying that you should stage this. In fact, as you can see, she *(indicating the STEPDAUGHTER)* is no longer that little girl with pigtails on her shoulders…

STEPDAUGHTER …and bloomers showing beneath her skirt!

FATHER Now comes the drama, sir. New, complex…

STEPDAUGHTER *(threatening, proud, moving forward)* …right after my father died…

FATHER *(interrupting, so as not to give her time to speak)* …poverty, sir! They came back here, without my knowing it. On account of her stupidity. *(indicating the MOTHER)* She barely knows how to write, but she could have had her daughter or the boy write to tell me that they were in need!

MOTHER Tell me, sir, how could I guess what his feelings were towards us?

FATHER That is exactly your problem. You have never understood any of my feelings!

MOTHER After so many years of separation and everything that had happened….

FATHER And is it my fault if that man took you all away? *(turning back to the DIRECTOR)* As I told you, from one day to the next… because he'd found some sort of job out of town…I lost track of them and then naturally had less interest in them for many years. The drama, unforeseen and violent, erupts when they return. I was, my God, driven by the misery of carnal desire…misery, yes misery, for a single man who doesn't want humiliating liaisons. Not old enough to do without women and not young enough to go after them easily and shamelessly. Misery — what am I saying? No, horror. Horror because no woman can give him love anymore. When you understand that, you should do without it. But heaven knows! On the outside, before others, everyone is clothed in dignity. Inside, however, we all acknowledge to ourselves the unmentionable things that go on. We give in, yes, we give in to temptation only to rise again immediately after, in great haste, to reconstruct our dignity into something integral and solid, like a tombstone over a grave that buries and hides — even from our own sight — all the signs and the memories of shame. And this is true of everyone! What we lack is the courage to say certain things.

STEPDAUGHTER But everyone has the courage to *do* them!

FATHER Yes, everyone! But secretly. It takes more courage to say them, because anyone who says them is forever dubbed a cynic. Whereas it's not true, sir. The one who says these things is no different from the others, in fact better than they are, because he is not afraid to reveal with the light of his intellect the red flush of shame in his own human bestiality when others close their eyes. Take a woman, for example. What does she do? She looks at a man, exciting him, inviting him. You grab her! As soon as you've got her, she closes her eyes. This is the sign that she is yielding, the sign by which she announces, "Blind yourself; I am blind!"

STEPDAUGHTER And when she no longer closes them? When she no longer feels the need to close her eyes, hiding from herself the red flush of her shame? Instead she sees — now dry-eyed and impassive — a man who, feeling no love for her, has blinded himself? Ha! All these intellectual complications, all these philosophical rationalizations that reveal the beast and then want to save it, excuse it. They make me sick! I can't stand listening to him, sir! Because when we have to "simplify" life that way, bestiality, throwing out the "human" impediments such as chaste aspirations, pure feelings, idealism, duties, modesty, shame, then nothing is more revolting and nauseating than certain kinds of remorse. Crocodile tears!

DIRECTOR Let's get to the action. Let's get to the facts, ladies and gentlemen. This is all just talk!

FATHER Yes, sir, that's true! But a fact is like an empty bag. When it's empty, it won't stand up. To make it stand up, you must first put into it the reason and the feelings that determined the fact. I had no way of knowing that when that man died, and they all came back here in dire poverty, she'd gone out looking for work to provide for her children *(indicating the MOTHER)*. And she found a job as a seamstress with that...that Madame Pace!

STEPDAUGHTER A high-class dressmaker, if you people are interested. She works in apparel for the finest ladies, but she arranged things so that those ladies served her purposes, masking her not-so-refined ladies.

MOTHER You must believe me, sir, if I tell you that I could never have suspected that the witch gave me work because she had her eye on my daughter....

STEPDAUGHTER Poor mamma! Do you know, sir, what that woman did as soon as I brought her the work that my mother had done? That woman showed me everything that was ruined because of my mother's sewing, and she deducted and deducted. So that, you see, I paid, while poor mamma thought she was sacrificing herself for me and for those two, sewing Madame Pace's stuff even at night! *(The ACTORS move about, expressing indignation.)*

DIRECTOR *(jumping in)* And there, one day, you met....

STEPDAUGHTER *(indicating the FATHER)* Yes sir, him, him! An old client! You'll see what a scene there is to be played. Superb!

FATHER With her mother's arrival...

STEPDAUGHTER *(interrupting, treacherously)* ...almost on time...!

FATHER *(screaming)* ...no, on time, on time! Because, luckily, I recognized her on time! And I brought them all to my house, sir. Now you can imagine my situation and hers, facing each other: her, as you see her, and me, who can no longer look her in the eye!

STEPDAUGHTER What a riot! But tell me, sir, how could he possibly expect me *now* to act like a modest, polite and virtuous young lady, conforming to his damnable aspirations to "solid moral health"?

FATHER For me, the whole drama lies in this, sir, in my awareness — in everyone's awareness, you see — of being "one" when in truth we are "many" — "many" according to the possibilities that lie within us. One with this person, one with that person, completely different! Yet we have the illusion of always being "one for all," and always "the one" that we believe ourselves to be in all of our actions. It's not true! It's not true! We realize this, when due to a single action, a great misfortune, we suddenly find ourselves as if caught on a hook and suspended on a pillory.

I mean, we realize that this act does not contain ourselves in our entirety and that it would be an atrocious injustice to judge us on that one act alone — to keep us hooked and suspended on the pillory for life, as though our entire existence could be summed up in that act. Now do you understand that girl's treachery? She caught me by surprise in a place, in an act and in a way that she should not have known me, in a way that for her I could not be. And she wants to give me a reality, one I could never expect to have for her, from a fleeting and shameful moment of my life! This is what hurts me the most. And this is what will make the drama great. Then there's also the others' situation! His.... *(He indicates the SON.)*

SON *(shrugging his shoulders in contempt)* Just leave me alone. I have nothing to do with it!

FATHER What do you mean you have nothing to do with it?

SON Nothing, and I want nothing to do with it, because as you well know I wasn't made to appear with the rest of you!

STEPDAUGHTER Because we're common people, and he's so refined! But you can see for yourself, sir. Every time I look at him to nail him with my contempt, he lowers his eyes — because he knows how he wronged me.

SON *(barely looking at her)* Me?

STEPDAUGHTER Yes, you. You! If I'm walking the streets, my dear, it's because of you! *(horrified gestures from the ACTORS)* Did you or didn't you, with your aloofness, make us feel, I won't say not-at-home, but unwelcome even as guests? We were the intruders coming to invade the kingdom of your *legitimacy.* Sir, I'd like to have you watch a few little scenes just between him and me! He says that I tyrannized everyone. But don't you see? It's precisely because of his aloofness that I had to make use of the event that he calls "vile." That is the reason I came into his home with my mother — who is also his mother — and took on the role of Mistress of the House!

SON *(moving forward slowly)* They've got all the advantages, sir, the easy roles, all ganging up on me. But imagine a son, living quietly at home, who one fine day sees a young woman come to his house. Brazen, cocky, with her nose in the air, she asks for his father, because she has something to tell him. Then he sees her come back, acting the same way, along with that little girl, and treating his father — who knows why? — in a most equivocal and brash manner, asking for money in a tone of voice that suggests that he must, must give it to her because he is obliged to do so —

FATHER But I *am* obliged to do so. For your mother!

SON And what do I know about her? When have I ever seen her? When have I ever heard her speak? One day, I see her appear with her *(indicates the STEPDAUGHTER)*, with that boy, with that little girl. They say to me: "Don't you know? She's your mother too!" I'm able to figure out from the way she acts *(indicating the STEPDAUGHTER again)* the reason why they just appeared at the house like that.... Sir, what I'm experiencing, what I'm feeling, I can't and don't want to express. At best, I could confide it to someone, but I wouldn't want to, even to myself. As you can see, then, my feelings can't give rise to any action on my part. Believe me, believe me, sir, I am a dramatically unrealized character, and I am uncomfortable, extremely uncomfortable, in their presence. Let them leave me alone!

FATHER What are you saying? Look here! It's because of you....

SON *(extremely exasperated)* And what do you know about me? When have you ever paid any attention to me?

FATHER True. I admit it! But isn't this a dramatic situation in itself? The way you isolate yourself, so cruel to me and to your mother. Returning home, she sees you grown up as if for the first time, not knowing you, but knowing that you are her son. *(indicating the MOTHER to the DIRECTOR)* Look at her. She's crying!

STEPDAUGHTER *(angrily, stamping her foot)* Like a fool!

FATHER *(quickly, indicating the STEPDAUGHTER to the DIRECTOR)* And we all know she can't stand him! *(referring to the SON again)* He says he has nothing to do with all this, and yet the action almost hinges on him! Look at that little boy, who always stays close to his mother, bewildered, humiliated.... He's like that because of him! Perhaps his situation is the most painful of all. He feels estranged, the poor boy, and anguished and mortified to be taken into my home out of charity.... *(confidentially)* He's exactly like his father! Humble, quiet....

DIRECTOR But that's no good! You have no idea what trouble it is to put kids on the stage.

FATHER Oh, he won't trouble you for very long, you know. The little girl too, she'll be the first to leave.

DIRECTOR Well, all right! I assure you that this whole story interests me. It interests me a great deal. I have a sense that great drama can be made from this material.

STEPDAUGHTER *(trying to cut in)* With a character like me!

FATHER *(pushing her aside, anxious to know the DIRECTOR's decision)* You be quiet!

DIRECTOR *(continuing, without paying attention to the interruption)* Something new, yes....

FATHER *Really* new, sir!

DIRECTOR It took a lot of guts, I'd say, to come in and pitch it to me as you did....

FATHER You must understand, sir, that since we were born for the stage....

DIRECTOR Are you amateur actors?

FATHER No, I say born for the stage because....

DIRECTOR Come on, you must have acted before!

FATHER Not at all, sir, or only in the sense that all of us play the parts that we've assigned ourselves or that others have assigned us in life. As for me, then, it's passion itself that becomes a bit theatrical, once I get worked up — as is true for everyone....

DIRECTOR Forget it. But you must understand, dear sir, that without an author...I could direct you to someone....

FATHER No need. Look here — what about you?

DIRECTOR Me? What are you saying?

FATHER Yes, you, you! Why not?

DIRECTOR Because I've never been an author!

FATHER But why couldn't you be one now? It doesn't take much. Everyone's doing it. Your job will be easier because we're here, alive, in front of you.

DIRECTOR But that's not enough!

FATHER Why not? Seeing us live out our drama....

DIRECTOR Sure! But you still need someone to write it!

FATHER No, just to transcribe it, because the action will be played right in front of you, scene by scene. At first it will be enough to do just a rough sketch — and then try it out.

DIRECTOR *(getting up on the stage again, tempted)* Well, I'm kind of tempted. Just for fun.... We could give it a try.

FATHER Of course, sir! You'll see what scenes will come out of it! I can tell you what they are right away.

DIRECTOR You tempt me, you tempt me. Let's give it a try. Come with me to my office. *(addresses the ACTORS)* You can take a break, but don't go far. Be back in fifteen or twenty minutes. *(to the FATHER)* Let's see, let's try...maybe something really extraordinary will come out of it.

FATHER No doubt about it! But don't you think they should come with us? *(indicates the other CHARACTERS)*

DIRECTOR Yes, come along, all of you. *(He starts to exit, then turns back to address the ACTORS.)* Don't forget, be on time! In fifteen minutes. *(The DIRECTOR and the SIX CHARACTERS cross the stage and disappear. The ACTORS remain onstage, as if stunned, looking at each other.)*

LEAD ACTOR Is he serious? What's he trying to do?

YOUNG ACTOR This is insane!

A THIRD ACTOR He wants us to improvise a play just like that, off the cuff?

YOUNG ACTOR Right! Like they used to do in the *commedia dell'arte.*

LEAD ACTRESS Ah, if he thinks that I'm going to take part in such jokes....

YOUNG ACTRESS I'm not having anything to do with it either.

A FOURTH ACTOR I'd like to know who those people are *(alluding to the CHARACTERS).*

THIRD ACTOR Who do you think? Lunatics or swindlers.

YOUNG ACTOR And he's listening to them?

YOUNG ACTRESS It's vanity! He wants to show he's an author!

LEAD ACTOR Unbelievable! If theater is going to be reduced to this...my friends...

A FIFTH ACTOR I think it's fun!

THIRD ACTOR Well, let's wait and see what comes of it.

And so, talking among themselves, the ACTORS leave the stage, some of them exiting through the rear door, others going back to their dressing rooms. The curtain stays raised. The play is interrupted for about twenty minutes.

A bell rings to announce that the play is about to continue. From the dressing rooms, the door and from the audience, the DIRECTOR, the STAGE MANAGER, the HEAD STAGEHAND, the PROMPTER and the PROP MAN return and — at the same time — the DIRECTOR and the SIX CHARACTERS return from his office. Once the house lights dim. The stage is lit as before.

DIRECTOR Let's get going. Are we all here? Pay attention now, we're about to begin. Head stagehand!

HEAD STAGEHAND Here I am!

DIRECTOR Put on the setting for the parlor. Two side flats and a backdrop with a door will do. Right away, I tell you!

While the DIRECTOR talks with the STAGE MANAGER, the PROP MAN and the ACTORS about the upcoming performance, The HEAD STAGEHAND runs to carry out the orders and sets up the scenery as indicated: two side flats and a backdrop with a door, all painted in pink and gold stripes.

DIRECTOR *(to the PROP MAN)* Go see if there's a day bed in the storeroom.

PROP MAN Yes, sir, there's that green one.

STEPDAUGHTER No, not green! It was yellow, flowered velveteen. Very big! Quite comfortable.

PROP MAN Well, there's nothing like that.

DIRECTOR It doesn't matter! Put out the one we have.

STEPDAUGHTER What do you mean, "it doesn't matter"? Madame Pace's famous chaise-longue!

DIRECTOR We're just rehearsing now! Please don't get involved in this. *(to the STAGE MANAGER)* See if you can find a cabinet, sort of long and low.

STEPDAUGHTER The table, the little mahogany table for the light-blue envelope!

STAGE MANAGER *(to the DIRECTOR)* There's that little gilded one.

DIRECTOR OK, get that one!

FATHER A large mirror.

STEPDAUGHTER And the screen! I have to have a screen. How can I manage otherwise?

STAGE MANAGER Yes ma'am, we have lots of screens. Don't worry.

DIRECTOR *(to the STEPDAUGHTER)* And then some hangers, right?

STEPDAUGHTER Yes, lots and lots.

DIRECTOR *(to the STAGE MANAGER)* Go see how many there are, and have them brought here.

STAGE MANAGER Yes, sir. I'll take care of it. *(He also runs to carry out the DIRECTOR's orders, and while the DIRECTOR continues to talk to the PROMPTER, and then with the CHARACTERS and the ACTORS, the STAGE MANAGER has the STAGEHANDS bring in the pieces of furniture he has pointed out, and he arranges them as he sees fit.)*

DIRECTOR *(to the PROMPTER)* In the meantime, you go to your spot. Look here. This is an outline of the scenes, act by act. *(He gives him a few sheets of paper.)* You're going to have to show some real skill.

PROMPTER Shorthand?

DIRECTOR *(happily surprised)* That's great! You know how to take shorthand?

PROMPTER I may not be much at prompting, but shorthand...!

DIRECTOR Better and better! *(addressing one of the STAGEHANDS)* Go get some paper from my office — piles of it — as much as you can find! *(The STAGEHAND runs out and comes back a little later with a big pile of paper, which he gives to the PROMPTER.)*

DIRECTOR *(to the PROMPTER again)* Follow the scenes carefully, as they are performed, and try to take down the lines, at least the most important ones! *(then, addressing the ACTORS)* Move over, everyone! Go to this side *(indicating stage left)* and pay close attention!

LEAD ACTRESS Excuse me, but we....

DIRECTOR *(anticipating her remark)* Don't worry, you won't have to improvise!

LEAD ACTOR So what do we have to do?

DIRECTOR Nothing! For now just listen and watch! Then you'll each have your written lines. Now we're going to rehearse as best we can. *They* are the ones who will do it! *(indicating the CHARACTERS)*

FATHER *(completely taken aback, in the midst of the confusion on stage)* We are going to rehearse? What does that mean?

DIRECTOR A rehearsal — a rehearsal for *them. (indicating the ACTORS)*

FATHER But we are the characters....

DIRECTOR Of course, the characters, but here, my dear sir, it's not the characters who perform, but the actors. The characters belong here, in the script *(he points to the prompter's box)* — when there is a script!

FATHER Exactly! Since there is no script, and you ladies and gentlemen have the good fortune to have live characters right here with you....

DIRECTOR Oh great! You'd like to do everything by yourselves? Act in front of the audience?

FATHER That's right. Just as we are.

DIRECTOR I can tell you that would be quite a show!

LEAD ACTOR And what would *we* have to do then?

DIRECTOR You people can't possibly think that you can act! You'd make everyone laugh.... *(The ACTORS, in fact, begin to laugh.)* There, you see, they're laughing! *(remembering)* Oh, more to the point, I've got to assign the parts. That's easy enough. They assign themselves. *(to the SUPPORTING ACTRESS)* You will play the MOTHER. *(to the FATHER)* We'll have to find a name for her.

FATHER Amalia, sir.

DIRECTOR But that's the name of your wife! We can't very well call her by her real name!

FATHER And why not, if that's her name...? But it's true, if it's going to be that lady...*(vaguely gestures toward the SUPPORTING ACTRESS)* I see *her (gesturing toward the MOTHER)* as Amalia, sir. But do as you like.... *(He becomes increasingly confused.)* I don't know what to say to you anymore. I'm starting to...I don't know, to hear my own words with a different sound, as though they were false.

DIRECTOR Don't worry. Don't worry about that at all! We'll help you find the right tone. As for the name, if you want "Amalia," "Amalia" it will be — or we'll find another name. For now, let's do the casting. *(to the YOUNG ACTOR)* You'll be the son. *(to the LEAD ACTRESS)* You, madam, of course, the stepdaughter.

STEPDAUGHTER *(excited)* What? What? I am...that woman? *(She bursts out laughing.)*

DIRECTOR *(irate)* What are you laughing about?

LEAD ACTRESS *(indignant)* No one has ever dared to laugh at me! Either you show me respect, or I'm leaving!

STEPDAUGHTER No, forgive me. I wasn't laughing at you.

DIRECTOR *(to the STEPDAUGHTER)* You should feel honored to be played by...

LEAD ACTRESS *(interrupting, with disdain)* ..."that woman!"

STEPDAUGHTER But I wasn't speaking of you, believe me! I was talking about myself, because I don't see myself in you at all. That's what I mean. I don't know...you're just not like me!

FATHER Yes, that's it. Don't you see, sir? Our expression....

DIRECTOR What do you mean, "your expression"? Do you think you have it in yourselves? Your expression? Not at all!

FATHER What? We can't express ourselves?

DIRECTOR Not at all! Here your expression becomes the raw material that the actors give body, shape, voice, and gesture to. And these actors, for your information, have been able to give expression to much greater material. Yours, on the other hand, is so slight that if it works on stage at all, the credit will go entirely to my actors.

FATHER I wouldn't dare contradict you, sir. But please understand that this will cause horrible suffering to us, who are as you see us, with these bodies, these looks....

DIRECTOR *(interrupting, impatient)* But we'll take care of the looks with make-up, my dear sir. We'll fix it all with make-up!

FATHER Well maybe, but what about voices, gestures?

DIRECTOR That's enough! Here you, as yourself, cannot exist. Here it's the actor who represents you, and that's it!

FATHER I understand, sir. But now perhaps I can guess why our author, who envisioned us alive as we are, didn't want to create us for the stage. I don't want to offend your actors. God forbid! But I think that seeing myself represented now...I don't know by whom....

LEAD ACTOR *(arrogantly rising and moving toward him, followed by giddy young ACTRESSES)* By me, with your permission.

FATHER *(humble, mellifluous)* Most honored, sir *(bowing)*. Yet it seems to me that no matter how hard this gentleman tries, with all his skill, to incorporate me into him.... *(He becomes confused.)*

LEAD ACTOR Get to the point. *(The ACTRESSES laugh.)*

FATHER *(to the DIRECTOR)* Well, what I mean is that his portrayal of me, even if he makes every effort to look like me, with make-up, I mean, shaped as he is...*(all the ACTORS laugh)* he can hardly show me as I really am. Instead it will be — apart from the way he looks — instead it will be how he interprets what I am. It will be how he senses me — if he senses me — and not how I sense myself from within. And it seems to me that whoever is called upon to judge us should take this into account.

DIRECTOR So now you're worried about what the critics will say? And I was standing here listening! Let the critics say what they want. Let's get busy putting this play together, if we can. *(moving away and looking around)* Come on, let's go. Is the set in order? *(to the ACTORS and CHARACTERS)* Get up! Out of the way. Let me see. *(stepping down off the stage)* Let's not waste any more time! *(to the STEPDAUGHTER)* Do you think the set's OK like that?

STEPDAUGHTER Well, to tell you the truth, I just don't see it.

DIRECTOR Enough! You can't expect that we're going to build Madame Pace's backroom, the one that you know, exactly as it was, for you! *(to the FATHER)* You told me a parlor with floral patterns.

FATHER Yes, sir. White.

DIRECTOR It's not white, it's striped, but it doesn't matter. As for the furniture, we're more or less set. That small table, bring it forward a little. *(The STAGEHANDS do so.) (to the PROP MAN)* And you in the meantime find an envelope, light blue if possible, and give it to this gentleman *(indicating the FATHER)*.

PROP MAN For a letter?

DIRECTOR AND FATHER For a letter. For a letter.

PROP MAN Right away! *(Exits.)*

DIRECTOR Come on, let's get going. The first scene is the one with the young lady. *(The LEAD ACTRESS steps forward.)* No, no, wait! I mean the young lady *(he indicates the STEPDAUGHTER)*. You just watch…

STEPDAUGHTER *(immediately adding)* …how I live it!

LEAD ACTRESS *(resentfully)* I'll be able to live it too, no doubt about it, as soon as I get into the role.

DIRECTOR *(hands on his head)* No more chitchat, please! So, the first scene is with the young lady and Madame Pace. Oh *(he becomes confused, looks around and goes back up onto the stage)*, and this Madame Pace?

FATHER She's not with us, sir.

DIRECTOR So what are we going to do?

FATHER But she's alive, she's alive too!

DIRECTOR OK, but where is she?

FATHER Just a minute. Let me say something. *(addressing the ACTRESSES)* If you ladies would do me the favor of giving me your hats for a while.

Actresses *(partly surprised, partly laughing, in chorus)* What? Our hats? What's he saying? Why? Oh, look!

DIRECTOR What do you want to do with the ladies' hats? *(The ACTORS laugh.)*

FATHER Oh nothing, just hang them on this coat rack for a moment. And if some of you ladies would be kind enough to take off your coats as well....

ACTORS *(as before)* Coats, too? What's next? He must be mad!

SOME ACTRESSES *(as before)* But why? Just coats?

FATHER To hang them up, just for a moment. Please do me this favor, will you?

ACTRESSES *(All taking off their hats and some their coats as well, they continue laughing while going to hang them here and there on the coat rack.)* And why not? Here you go! This is really getting funny. Are we supposed to put them on display?

FATHER Yes, exactly, madam. To put them on display, just like that!

DIRECTOR Would you tell us why?

FATHER I'll tell you why, sir. Maybe, if we set the stage better for her so that she is attracted by the very tools of her trade, who knows if she won't come to us.... *(indicating that everyone should look toward the rear exit)* Look! Look!

The rear exit opens and MADAME PACE takes a few steps forward. She is enormously fat, wearing an outrageous, carrot-colored wig made of wool with a flamboyant red rose on one side, in the Spanish style. Heavily made-up, she is dressed with clumsy elegance in garish red silk. She holds a feather fan in one hand while raising the other with a lighted cigarette between two fingers. When she appears, the ACTORS and the DIRECTOR run from the stage with cries of horror, hurrying down the stairs and attempting to get away through the aisle.

The STEPDAUGHTER*, on the other hand, runs up to* MADAME PACE*, submissive, as though in the presence of her mistress.*

STEPDAUGHTER *(running up to her)* Here she is! Here she is!

FATHER *(beaming)* It's Madame Pace herself! Didn't I tell you? Here she is!

DIRECTOR *(overcoming his initial astonishment, indignant)* What kind of trick is this? *(The next four lines are spoken almost at the same time as the* DIRECTOR*'s line.)*

LEAD ACTOR What on earth is going on?

YOUNG ACTOR Where did that one come from?

YOUNG ACTRESS They were keeping her in reserve.

LEAD ACTRESS This is all smoke and mirrors!

FATHER *(silencing their protests)* Listen, please! Why do you want to spoil, in the name of a vulgar, factual truth, this marvel of a reality being born, evoked, attracted and created by the stage set itself — a marvel that has more right to live here than you do, because it is far truer than you are? Which actress among you will play the role of Madame Pace? Well, *this* is Madame Pace! Grant me that the actress who plays her will be less true than she is — Madame Pace in person! Just look. My daughter has recognized her and gone right up to her. Wait and see. Watch the scene!

Hesitating, the DIRECTOR *and the* ACTORS *go back up on the stage. But the scene between the* STEPDAUGHTER *and* MADAME PACE *— during the* ACTORS*' protests and the* FATHER*'s rebuttal — has already begun. It is played sottovoce, naturally, in a way that would be impossible on stage. Thus, when the* ACTORS*, called to attention by the* FATHER*, turn around to look, they see* MADAME PACE*, who has already put her hand under the* STEPDAUGHTER*'s chin to make her lift her head. Hearing her speak unintelligibly, they pay attention for a moment but then become frustrated.*

DIRECTOR Well?

LEAD ACTOR What's she saying?

LEAD ACTRESS You can't hear a thing!

YOUNG ACTOR Louder! Louder!

STEPDAUGHTER *(walking away from MADAME PACE — who is smiling in her priceless way — and coming toward the group of ACTORS)* "Louder!" What do you mean, "louder"? These aren't things that can be said out loud! I could say them loudly to him *(indicates the FATHER)* to shame him, for my revenge! But for madame it's something else — prison!

DIRECTOR Oh, great! So that's the way it is? But here, my dear girl, you have to make yourself heard! We can't even hear you on the stage! Just imagine what it would be like for an audience in the theater! Now, you've got to do the scene. Anyway, you can speak out loud between yourselves, because we're not going to be here listening. Just pretend to be alone, in a room, in the back room, where no one can hear you. *(The STEPDAUGHTER, charmingly, but smiling maliciously, moves her finger back and forth to signal "no.")*

DIRECTOR What do you mean, "no"?

STEPDAUGHTER *(sottovoce, mysteriously)* There's someone who can hear us, sir, if she *(indicating MADAME PACE)* speaks loudly!

DIRECTOR *(very worried)* Is someone else going to jump out? *(The ACTORS prepare to escape from the stage again.)*

FATHER No, no, sir. She's referring to me. I have to be there, behind that door, waiting, and madame knows it. In fact, with your permission, I'll go get ready right now. *(He starts to move.)*

DIRECTOR *(stopping him)* No, wait! Here we must respect the demands of the theater! Before you're ready....

STEPDAUGHTER *(interrupting him)* Right away! Right now! I'm dying, I tell you, dying of my longing to live it, to live that scene! If he's going to be ready now, I'm more than ready!

DIRECTOR *(shouting)* But first the scene between you and that woman *(indicating MADAME PACE)* must come out loud and clear! Will you try to understand?

STEPDAUGHTER Oh my God! She told me what you already know. Mamma's work was badly done again, her stuff was ruined, and I must be patient if I want her to keep helping us in our poverty.

MADAME PACE *(moving forward with a look of great importance)* Eh, señor; porqué yo not quero profit, nó avantageo.

DIRECTOR *(almost afraid)* What? What? Is that the way she speaks? *(All the ACTORS burst out laughing uproariously.)*

STEPDAUGHTER *(also laughing)* Yes, sir, that's how she speaks, part Spanish, part English — quite funny!

MADAME PACE Ah, not nice you laugh at me, if I try hablar como can, in English, señor!

DIRECTOR No, not at all! Talk like that. Talk like that, madame! It'll have just the right effect! The perfect way to give some comic relief to the harshness of the situation. Speak just like that! It's wonderful!

STEPDAUGHTER Wonderful! How could it not be? To hear certain propositions made to you in a language like that — it has the right effect, because it almost seems like a joke, sir! It makes you laugh when you hear her say that there's an "old señor" who wants to "amuse himself with migo." Right, madame?

MADAME PACE Not old, linda, viejito, a little old. But mejor para ti: you don'ta like him, but he give prudencia!

MOTHER *(rising, amidst the astonishment and consternation of all the ACTORS, who were not paying attention to her and who now respond to her shouting by rushing over to restrain her. They are also laughing because, in the meantime, she has pulled off MADAME PACE's wig and thrown it to the ground.)* Witch! Witch! Murderer! My daughter!

STEPDAUGHTER *(running up to restrain the MOTHER)* No, no, Mamma! I beg you.

FATHER *(running up at the same time)* Relax. Calm down. Sit down!

MOTHER Then get her away from me!

STEPDAUGHTER *(to the DIRECTOR, who has also run up)* It's impossible. It's impossible for mamma to be here!

FATHER *(also to the DIRECTOR)* They can't be together! That's the reason, you see, why that woman wasn't with us when we came here! If they're together, you see, the plot is given away too soon.

DIRECTOR It doesn't matter! It doesn't matter! For now it's like a rough draft. Everything is useful for getting the various elements together, even if they're all confused. *(He turns to the MOTHER and guides her back to her seat.)* Come, come, my dear lady, settle down. Go back to your seat. *(In the meantime the STEPDAUGHTER, going back to her scene, turns to MADAME PACE.)*

STEPDAUGHTER Come, madame, let's get on with it.

MADAME PACE *(offended)* Ah no, much gracias! Aquí I do nada with your mamma presenta.

STEPDAUGHTER Now, now, let that old *señor* in to have a good time *con migo. (turning to everyone, imperiously)* I tell you that scene has to be played! Come on, let's get on with it! *(to MADAME PACE)* You may leave!

MADAME PACE Ah, I go, I go, I go seguramente.... *(She exits, furious, picking up her wig and gazing haughtily at the ACTORS, who applaud while laughing scornfully.)*

STEPDAUGHTER *(to the FATHER)* Now you make your entrance! You don't need to go around! Come right over here! Pretend that you've just entered! Look. I'm standing here with my head lowered, modest! Come on now, speak up! Say to me, in a different voice, like someone who has just come from outside, "Good morning, miss...."

DIRECTOR *(already down off the stage)* Look here! Are you directing or am I? *(to the FATHER, who is watching him, uncertain and perplexed)* Go ahead. Yes. Back there, without exiting, and then come forward. *(The FATHER follows the directions, almost dumbfounded. He is extremely pale, but — already immersed in the reality of his created life — he smiles as he hurries forward, as if still estranged from the drama that is about to strike him down. The ACTORS suddenly pay close attention to the scene as it begins.)*

DIRECTOR *(softly, in a hurry, to the PROMPTER in his box)* And you, pay attention, get ready to write, now!

The Scene

FATHER *(walking up, in a different voice)* Good morning, miss.

STEPDAUGHTER *(head bowed, containing her disgust)* Good morning.

FATHER *(peering underneath her hat, which almost hides her face, and discovering that she is very young, exclaims almost to himself, partly out of delight and partly out of fear of compromising himself in a risky situation)* Ah...well...I mean, this isn't the first time you've come here, right?

STEPDAUGHTER *(as above)* No, sir.

FATHER You've been here before? *(The STEPDAUGHTER nods "yes.")* More than once? *(He waits a little for the answer, goes back to observing her under her hat, then smiles and says)* Well then… you shouldn't act like this any more.… Would you allow me to remove your hat?

STEPDAUGHTER *(quickly, to forestall him, no longer containing her disgust)* No, sir. I'll take it off myself! *(She does so in a hurry, trembling. The MOTHER, watching the scene with the SON and her TWO CHILDREN, younger and more bonded to her, remains on the opposite side of the stage from the ACTORS. As though on pins and needles, she follows the words and actions of the FATHER and STEPDAUGHTER with varying expressions — of pain, of scorn, of anxiety, of horror. At times she hides her face, at other times she lets out a moan.)*

MOTHER My God! My God!

FATHER *(On hearing her moan, he pauses as if turned to stone for a moment, then he speaks as before.)* That's right. Give it to me. I'll put it down. *(He takes the hat from her hands.)* But on such a lovely, dear little head as yours, I'd like to see a hat more worthy of it. Wouldn't you like to help me choose some from these that belong to Madame Pace? No?

YOUNG ACTRESS *(interrupting)* Hey, watch out! Those are our hats!

DIRECTOR *(suddenly, furious)* Quiet, for God's sake! Don't try to be funny! This is the scene! *(addressing the STEPDAUGHTER)* Go on, please.

STEPDAUGHTER *(resuming)* No thank you, sir.

FATHER Oh, come on. Don't say no to me! You must accept it, or my feelings will be hurt. There are some very pretty ones. Just look! And then we'd also make madame happy. She displays them here on purpose!

STEPDAUGHTER No, sir. You see, I couldn't even wear one.

FATHER Maybe you mean because of what they'd say at home if they saw you coming back with a new hat? Don't worry! Do you know how to handle that? What to say at home?

STEPDAUGHTER *(impatient, unable to stand it anymore)* But it's not because of that, sir! I couldn't wear it, because I'm...as you see me. You might have already noticed! *(She indicates her black outfit.)*

FATHER In mourning, of course! Excuse me. It's true. I see. I beg your pardon. Believe me. I'm very sorry.

STEPDAUGHTER *(making an effort to find the courage to overcome her indignation and disgust)* That's OK, sir! I'm the one who should be thanking you. You have no need to be sorry or embarrassed. Don't even think about what I said, please. Even for myself, you see *(she forces herself to smile and adds)* I can't think about the way I'm dressed.

DIRECTOR *(interrupting, addressing the PROMPTER and climbing back on the stage)* Wait, wait! Stop writing. Leave out that last sentence. Leave it out! *(Addressing the FATHER and the STEPDAUGHTER)* It's terrific! Terrific! *(then to the FATHER alone)* And here you'll say your lines as we planned! *(to the ACTORS)* Delightful, this little scene with the hat, don't you think?

STEPDAUGHTER But the best part is coming now! Why don't we go on?

DIRECTOR Be patient just for a moment! *(addressing the ACTORS again)* Naturally it has to be played rather lightly.

LEAD ACTOR Easy does it....

LEAD ACTRESS Of course. Nothing to it! *(to the LEAD ACTOR)* We can rehearse it right away, can't we?

LEAD ACTOR Sure. Here. I'll turn around to make my entrance! *(He exits to be ready to re-enter through the backdrop door.)*

DIRECTOR *(to the LEAD ACTRESS)* So then, look here. The scene between you and Madame Pace has ended — I'll take care of writing it later on. You stay.... No, where are you going?

LEAD ACTRESS Wait. I'm putting on my hat again. *(She does so, taking her hat off the rack.)*

DIRECTOR Oh you're right. Very good! OK, you stand here with your head bowed.

STEPDAUGHTER *(amused)* But she's not dressed in black!

LEAD ACTRESS I will be dressed in black, and much more effectively than you!

DIRECTOR *(to the STEPDAUGHTER)* Be quiet, please! Stay still and watch! You'll learn something! *(clapping his hands)* Go ahead. Go ahead! The entrance!

He climbs down again from the stage to get an impression of the scene. The back door opens and the LEAD ACTOR steps forward with the roguish, free-and-easy manner of an ageing libertine. The ACTORS' performance of the scene should seem from the first lines something different, without giving the slightest impression of a parody. Rather, it should appear embellished. Naturally, the STEPDAUGHTER and the FATHER, not being able to recognize themselves at all in the LEAD ACTRESS and the LEAD ACTOR when they hear them pronounce their own words, express in various ways — gestures, smiles, open protests — their impressions of surprise, wonder, suffering, etc., as indicated below. The PROMPTER's voice is clearly heard from his box.

LEAD ACTOR "Good morning, miss...."

FATHER *(instantly, unable to contain himself)* No, no! *(The STEPDAUGHTER, seeing the way the LEAD ACTOR makes his entrance, bursts out laughing at the same time.)*

DIRECTOR *(furious)* Be quiet, both of you! And you, once and for all, stop laughing! We can't go on like this!

STEPDAUGHTER *(coming from the proscenium)* I'm sorry, sir, but it's perfectly natural! This lady *(indicating the LEAD ACTRESS)* just stands still, in her place, but if she's supposed to be me, I can assure you that if I heard someone say "good morning" to me in that way and that tone of voice, I would burst out laughing, just as I did now!

FATHER *(also coming forward a little)* Yes, indeed...the manner, the tone....

DIRECTOR What manner? What tone? Now, move over and let me watch the rehearsal!

LEAD ACTOR *(moving forward)* If I'm supposed to be playing an old man coming into a house of ill repute....

DIRECTOR Of course, pay no attention to them, for heaven's sake! Take it from the top; it was going just fine! *(Waiting for the LEAD ACTOR to begin)* So....

LEAD ACTOR "Good morning, miss...."

LEAD ACTRESS "Good morning...."

LEAD ACTOR *(imitating the FATHER's gesture of looking underneath her hat, but then expressing very distinctly first delight and then fear)* "Ah...well...I mean, this isn't the first time, I hope...."

FATHER *(correcting, irresistibly)* Not "I hope." "Right?" "Right?"

DIRECTOR He says, "Right, question mark."

LEAD ACTOR *(pointing to the PROMPTER)* I heard, "I hope!"

DIRECTOR OK, it's the same thing! "Right," or "I hope." Go on, go on. Well, maybe a little less heavy handed.... Here, I'll play it for you. Just watch. *(He goes back on stage, playing the part from the beginning.)* "Good morning, miss...."

LEAD ACTRESS "Good morning."

DIRECTOR "Ah...well...I mean...." *(addressing the LEAD ACTOR to make him notice the way he looks at the LEAD ACTRESS from underneath her hat)* Surprise...fear and delight.... *(then continuing, to the LEAD ACTRESS)* "This isn't the first time, right? That you've come here...." *(again addressing the LEAD ACTOR with a knowing look)* Is that clear? *(to the LEAD ACTRESS)* Now you say, "No, sir." *(again to the LEAD ACTOR)* Briefly — how shall I put it — lightly, with finesse! *(He goes back down off the stage.)*

LEAD ACTRESS "No, sir...."

LEAD ACTOR "You've been here before? More than once?"

DIRECTOR No, no! Wait till she *(indicating the LEAD ACTRESS)* nods "yes." "More than once?" *(The LEAD ACTRESS raises her head a little, closing her eyes as if in disgust, and then, when the DIRECTOR says "Down," she lowers her head twice.)*

STEPDAUGHTER *(irresistibly)* Oh, my God! *(She puts her hand over her mouth to contain her laughter.)*

DIRECTOR *(turning around)* What's the matter?

STEPDAUGHTER *(instantly)* Nothing, nothing!

DIRECTOR *(to the LEAD ACTOR)* Your cue, go ahead!

LEAD ACTOR More than once? Well then…you shouldn't act like this anymore.… Would you allow me to remove your hat? *(He says this last line in such a tone, along with such a movement, that the STEPDAUGHTER — her hand still on her mouth — as much as she tries to stop herself, can't contain the loud laughter that inevitably escapes through her fingers.)*

LEAD ACTRESS *(indignant, going back to her seat)* Ha! I'm not going to stand here and play the fool for that girl.

LEAD ACTOR Neither am I! Let's call it quits.

DIRECTOR *(to the STEPDAUGHTER, screaming)* Stop it! Stop it!

STEPDAUGHTER Yes. Forgive me, Forgive me.

DIRECTOR You're rude. That's what you are! And arrogant!

FATHER *(trying to intervene)* Yes, sir. It's true. It's true. But forgive her.

DIRECTOR *(going back on stage)* And why should I forgive her! It's indecent!

FATHER Yes, sir. But believe me, believe me, it has such a strange effect on us.…

DIRECTOR Strange? What do you mean, "strange"? Why strange?

FATHER I admire them, sir, I admire your actors. This gentleman *(indicates the LEAD ACTOR)*, this lady *(indicates the LEAD ACTRESS)*, but, of course…well, they are not us.…

DIRECTOR Of course not! How could they be you, if they are actors?

FATHER That's just it, they're actors! And they play our parts well, both of them. But believe me when I tell you that it seems like something very different to us, something that should be the same, but isn't!

DIRECTOR But how is it not the same? What is it then?

FATHER It's something that…becomes theirs and is no longer ours.

DIRECTOR But that's the way it is! I've already told you so.

FATHER Yes, I understand, I understand.…

DIRECTOR So that's that. Enough! *(addressing the ACTORS)* This means that we'll rehearse by ourselves, as we should. It's always been a curse for me to rehearse in front of authors! They're never satisfied! *(addressing the FATHER and the STEPDAUGHTER)* OK, let's take it again with you two, and let's see if it's possible for you not to laugh.

STEPDAUGHTER Oh, I won't laugh any more. I won't laugh any more. The best part for me is coming now. You can be sure!

DIRECTOR So, when you say, "Don't even think about what I said, please...even for myself, you see..." *(addressing the FATHER)* you have to say your line right away: "I understand. I understand...." and then immediately ask...

STEPDAUGHTER *(interrupting)* What? What does he ask?

DIRECTOR The reason you're in mourning.

STEPDAUGHTER No, sir, that's not it! Look. When I told him that I can't think about the way I'm dressed, do you know what he said? "Ah, very good! Then let's take it off. Let's take it off, right now, this little dress!"

DIRECTOR Oh great! Terrific! Do you want to explode the whole theater?

STEPDAUGHTER But it's the truth.

DIRECTOR What do you mean the truth? Give me a break! We're in the theater! Truth, up to a certain point!

STEPDAUGHTER So, what do you intend to do then?

DIRECTOR You'll see! You'll see! Let me handle things now!

STEPDAUGHTER No, sir! Using my disgust and all the reasons — one more cruel and vile than the next — why I am as I am, you would like to piece together a sentimental little romantic story, with him asking me the reason I'm in mourning and me answering, with tears in my eyes, that my Papa died two months ago? No, no, my dear sir! He has to say to me exactly what he said, "Then let's take it off right now, this little dress!" And I, with my heart in mourning for just two months, I went over there, you see? There, behind that screen, and with these fingers trembling with shame, with horror, I took off my dress, unhooked my corset....

DIRECTOR *(running his hands through his hair)* For God's sake, what are you saying?

STEPDAUGHTER *(screaming, frantic)* The truth! The truth, sir!

DIRECTOR Of course, I don't deny it. It may be the truth...and I understand, I understand all your horror, but you must also understand that all this isn't possible on the stage!

STEPDAUGHTER Not possible? OK. Well, thanks, but count me out.

DIRECTOR Now look here....

STEPDAUGHTER Count me out! Count me out! What's possible on the stage was contrived by the two of you, over there. Thank you. I get it! He wants to go directly to the staging of *(with emphasis)* his *spiritual torment.* But I want to act out my drama, mine!

DIRECTOR *(annoyed, shrugging haughtily)* Oh, *yours,* of course. Excuse me, but your drama isn't the only one! There are those of the others, too! His *(indicating the FATHER),* your mother's! We can't let one character upstage all the others, taking over everything. What we have to do is fit them all into the right framework and perform what is performable! I know as well as you that all of them have complete inner lives that they would like to display. But the hard part is this: to display just what is necessary in relation to the others and yet with that little bit to suggest the whole other life that remains inside! Sure, it would be nice if each character could, with a long monologue, or even better, with a lecture, dish out in front of the audience everything that's boiling in his pot! *(in a kindly, conciliatory tone)* You must control yourself, young lady. And believe me, it's in your own interest because — I'm warning you — you could give a bad impression with all that explosive anger, that exasperated disgust. You yourself — I'm sorry — have confessed to being with other men before you were with him at Madame Pace's, and more than once!

STEPDAUGHTER *(lowering her head, speaking in a hushed voice, after a moment of reflection)* It's true! But, you see, for me all the others are him as well!

DIRECTOR *(not understanding)* All the others? What do you mean?

STEPDAUGHTER For those who fall into sin, sir, isn't the one who caused the fall responsible for all the sins that follow? For me, he's the one, even before I was born. Look at him and see if it's not true!

DIRECTOR Oh, wonderful! And do you think he carries the weight of his remorse lightly? Let him display it!

STEPDAUGHTER And just how could he show all his *noble* feelings of remorse, all his *moral* torments, if you want to spare him the horror of having found in his arms, one fine day — after asking her to take off her mourning dress — an already fallen woman? That little girl, yes, sir, that little girl that he used to go see as she was coming out of school? *(She says these last words in a voice trembling with emotion. The MOTHER, hearing her say these things, is overcome by a surge of uncontrollable anxiety, which she expresses first in a few muffled sobs and finally in an outburst of weeping. Everyone is overcome with sympathy. Long pause. As soon as the MOTHER begins to quiet down, the STEPDAUGHTER adds, in a somber and resolute tone)* Here, now. We're by ourselves, still unknown to an audience. Tomorrow you'll put on whatever show you like about us, orchestrating it in your own way. But do you want to see the real drama unfold as it actually did?

DIRECTOR Of course. I couldn't ask for anything better, so that I can use as much of it as I can, starting now!

STEPDAUGHTER OK, then have my mother exit.

MOTHER *(rising from her tears with a loud cry)* No. No, don't allow it, sir. Don't allow it!

DIRECTOR But, madam, it's just to see!

MOTHER I can't! I can't!

DIRECTOR But if everything has already happened... I'm sorry. I don't understand!

MOTHER No, it's happening now. It happens all the time! My suffering is not over, sir! I am alive and present always, in every moment of my suffering. It always renews itself. It's always alive and present. Those two little ones. Have you heard them speak? They can't speak any more, sir! They still cling to me to keep my suffering alive and present, but they, for themselves, no longer exist! And this one *(indicating the STEPDAUGHTER)*, sir, ran away, escaped from me, and is lost, completely lost.... If I still see her here, it's just for that reason, always, always, only for this: to keep renewing, alive and present, the pain that I suffered for her as well!

FATHER *(solemnly)* The eternal moment, as I told you, sir! She *(indicating the STEPDAUGHTER)* is here to seize me, to immobilize me, leave me eternally hooked and suspended on the pillory in that unique fleeting and shameful moment of my life. She can't stop it and you, sir, can't really spare me from it.

DIRECTOR Of course, I fully intend to stage it. In fact, it will form the nucleus of the whole first act, up to her *(indicates the MOTHER)* surprise entrance.

FATHER Yes, that's right. Because it's my doom, sir. All our passion, which must culminate in her final cry! *(also indicating the MOTHER)*

STEPDAUGHTER I can still hear it! That cry drove me crazy! You can put me on stage as you like, sir. It doesn't matter! Even dressed. As long as at least my arms — only my arms — are bare, because, you see, standing like this *(she goes up to the FATHER and leans her head on his chest),* with my head against him like this and my arms like this, around his neck, I saw a vein pulsing here on my arm and then, as if it were only that live vein that disgusted me, I squinted like this, like this, and buried my head in his chest! *(turning towards the MOTHER)* Scream, mamma, scream! *(She buries her head in the FATHER's chest, and with her shoulders raised as if to block out the cry, she adds, in an agonized, hushed voice)* Scream, like you screamed then!

MOTHER *(rushing up to separate them)* No! My daughter! My daughter! *(and after pulling her away from him)* Brute! You brute. That's my daughter! Can't you see she's my daughter?

DIRECTOR *(At her cry, he backs up all the way to the front of the stage amid the ACTORS' consternation)* Wonderful! Yes, terrific! And now, curtain, curtain!

FATHER *(running up to him, agitated)* Yes, of course, because that's how it really was, sir!

DIRECTOR *(admiring and convinced)* Yes, yes, here, no doubt! Curtain! Curtain! *(Hearing the DIRECTOR cry "curtain" several times, the HEAD STAGEHAND lowers the curtain, leaving the DIRECTOR and the FATHER at the front of the stage.)*

DIRECTOR *(gazing upward with his arms raised)* What idiocy! I say "curtain," meaning that the act should end here, and they lower the curtain for real! *(To the FATHER, lifting an edge of the curtain in order to return to the stage)* Yes, yes, it's really good! Sure-fire effect! That's how it has to end. I guarantee, I guarantee this first act! *(He re-enters with the FATHER.)*

When the curtain opens again, it is apparent that the STAGEHANDS have taken down the sketchy scenery for the first act and set up in its place a small garden pool. The ACTORS are seated in a row on one side of the stage and the CHARACTERS on the other. The DIRECTOR is standing, center stage, his fist to his mouth, meditating.

DIRECTOR *(shrugging after a brief pause)* All right, we come to the second act. Leave it to me, as we agreed earlier, and everything will be fine!

STEPDAUGHTER Our arrival at his house *(indicates the FATHER)* in spite of *him (indicates the SON)!*

DIRECTOR *(exasperated)* OK, but I tell you, leave it to me!

STEPDAUGHTER As long as his spite is made clear!

MOTHER *(from her side, shaking her head)* For all the good that came from it....

STEPDAUGHTER *(whirling towards her)* It doesn't matter! The more damage to us, the more remorse for him!

DIRECTOR *(exasperated)* I get it! I get it! And we'll take this into account, especially at the beginning! Don't worry!

MOTHER *(pleading)* But make it so they understand, I beg you, sir, for my conscience, that I tried as best I could...

STEPDAUGHTER *(interrupting her scornfully, and continuing)* ...to calm me down, to encourage me not to act spitefully towards him! *(to the DIRECTOR)* You can satisfy her. Satisfy her in this, because it's true! I'll really enjoy it, because that way everyone will see that the more she pleads, the more she tries to gain his affection, the more that boy keeps his distance: *ab-sent!* What fun!

DIRECTOR Shall we finally begin this second act?

STEPDAUGHTER I'll stop talking! But watch out. Making the whole thing take place in the garden — as you want to do — won't work!

DIRECTOR And why not?

STEPDAUGHTER Because he *(indicating the SON again)* always stays shut up in his room, isolated! And then, the part involving that poor boy there, the lost one, has to take place in the house, as I told you.

DIRECTOR Maybe so! But on the other hand, you'll all have to understand that we can't very well put up signs or change scenery in plain sight three or four times per act!

LEAD ACTOR It used to be done, once....

DIRECTOR Sure, when the spectators were about the age of that little girl!

LEAD ACTRESS And creating illusion was easier!

FATHER *(jumping up)* Illusion? For heaven's sake, please don't say "illusion"! Don't use that word, which for us is especially cruel!

DIRECTOR *(stunned)* And why not, pray tell?

FATHER It's cruel, cruel! You should be able to understand that!

DIRECTOR What should we say, then? The illusion to be created, here, for the audience...

LEAD ACTOR ...by our performance...

DIRECTOR ...the illusion of reality!

FATHER I understand, sir. But perhaps you're the one who can't understand us. Forgive me! Because — you see — for you and your actors here, it's simply a question of — as it should be — a game.

LEAD ACTRESS *(interrupting, indignant)* What do you mean, a game? We're not children! We take our acting seriously here.

FATHER I don't deny it. What I mean is the game of your art, which is supposed to create — exactly as the director said — a perfect illusion of reality.

DIRECTOR Yes, exactly!

FATHER Now, imagine that we ourselves *(indicating himself and the other five CHARACTERS)* have no reality outside of this illusion!

DIRECTOR *(stunned, looking at his ACTORS who also seem shocked and bewildered)* And what do you mean?

FATHER *(after observing them for a while, with a faint smile)* Of course, ladies and gentlemen! What else is there? What for you is an illusion to be created is for us our only reality. *(Brief pause. He moves several steps toward the DIRECTOR and adds)* But not only for us. Think about it. *(He looks the DIRECTOR in the eye.)* Can you tell me who you are? *(He continues to point his index finger at him.)*

DIRECTOR *(disturbed, with a half-smile)* What do you mean, who am I? I'm myself!

FATHER And if I told you that isn't true, because you're me?

DIRECTOR I'd say that you're crazy! *(The ACTORS laugh.)*

FATHER You're right to laugh, because you're playing here. *(to the DIRECTOR)* You can therefore argue with me that it's only because it's a game that this gentleman *(indicates the LEAD ACTOR)*, who is *himself*, is supposed to be *me*, who, on the other hand, am myself. Do you see that I've caught you in a trap? *(The ACTORS start laughing again.)*

DIRECTOR *(annoyed)* But that has already been pointed out. Are we starting over again?

FATHER No, no. That's not really what I wanted to say. Instead, I'd like to suggest that you step out of this game *(looking at the LEAD ACTRESS as if to forestall her)* of art! — of art! — the game that you are used to playing here with your actors, and I'll come back to asking you seriously, who are you?

DIRECTOR *(addressing the ACTORS, almost astounded and at the same time irritated)* Well, that takes a lot of nerve! A guy, who's passing himself off as a character, coming to ask me who I am!

FATHER *(with dignity, but not with arrogance)* A character, sir, can always ask a man who he is, because a character really has a life of his own, marked by his own characteristics, and because of this he's always "someone." Whereas a man — I'm not talking about you, now — a man, generally speaking, could be nobody.

DIRECTOR Ok. But you're asking *me* that question, and I'm the director! The head of the troupe! Do you understand?

FATHER *(very sweetly and humbly)* I just want to know, sir, if you, as you are today, can really see yourself.... How do you see, for example, with the distance of time, what you once were, with all the illusions you had then? How did things inside you and around you seem to you then? What were they, what were they really for you? Well then, thinking about those illusions that you no longer have, about all those things that no longer appear to you what they once were, don't you feel that the earth itself, the ground under your feet — I don't mean the boards on this stage — is no longer solid? Don't you reason that the person you feel yourself to be today, in all his present reality, is destined to seem to you an illusion tomorrow?

DIRECTOR *(not understanding, confused by the specious argument)* Well? Where are you going with this?

FATHER Oh, nowhere, sir. I'm just trying to make you see that if we *(again indicating himself and the other CHARACTERS)* have no other reality beyond illusion, it would also behoove you to distrust your reality, the one you breathe and feel in yourself today, because — like yesterday's — it is destined to reveal itself to be an illusion tomorrow.

DIRECTOR *(deciding to take it as a joke)* Wonderful! And now I suppose you're going to add that, with this play that you've come to put on for me here, you are truer and more real than I am!

FATHER *(with utmost seriousness)* No doubt about it, sir.

DIRECTOR Really?

FATHER I thought that you had understood this from the beginning.

DIRECTOR More real than I am?

FATHER If your reality can change from one day to the next...?

DIRECTOR Of course it can change! It changes continuously, like everyone else's.

FATHER *(shouting)* But ours doesn't, sir! Don't you see? That is the difference! It doesn't change. It can't change, it can never be otherwise, because it has been determined as *this* — forever — and it's a terrible thing, sir! —this immutable reality that should make all of you shudder when you approach us.

DIRECTOR *(Suddenly, struck by an idea that has just come to him, he stops in front of the FATHER.)* But I'd like to know when in the world anyone has ever seen a character step out of his role and then defend it as you are doing. Promote it. Explain it. Can you tell me? I've never seen it!

FATHER You have never seen it, sir, because usually authors hide the labor pains involved in their creations. When characters are alive, truly alive in front of their author, the author does nothing but observe the actions, words and gestures, which they propose to him, and he has to will them to be as they wish, or else! When a character is born, he immediately acquires such independence from his own author that everyone can imagine him in all kinds of situations where the author never thought of putting him. And sometimes he can also take on a meaning that the author never dreamed of giving him!

DIRECTOR Yes, of course. I know that!

FATHER Well then, why are you so astonished by us? Just imagine how wretched it is for a character who was born alive from the imagination of an author who then decided to deny him life. Then tell me if this character, so abandoned, alive yet without a life, isn't justified in doing what we are doing now, here before all of you. For a long time — a long time, believe me — we did the same thing with our author, appearing before him to persuade him, to push him, sometimes me, sometimes her *(indicating the STEPDAUGHTER)*, sometimes that poor mother....

STEPDAUGHTER *(stepping up, as if lost in thought)* It's true. I went too, sir. I went to tempt him, so many times, in the gloom of his study, at twilight. He would be lying back in an armchair, unable to make up his mind whether to turn on the light or let darkness invade the room — a darkness swarming with us, who had come to tempt him. *(as if she could still see herself in that study, and then bothered by the presence of all the ACTORS)* If you all would just go away! If you would leave us alone! Mamma there, with her son, me with that little girl, that boy there always alone, and then me with him *(gesturing towards the FATHER)*, and then me, myself, alone, alone — in that darkness. *(startled all of a sudden, as if she wanted to grasp the vision she has of herself, alive and shining in that darkness)* Ah, my life! What scenes! What scenes we went to propose to him! *I* tempted him more than anyone else!

FATHER True! But maybe it was all because of you. Because you insisted too many times. Because you could never control yourself!

STEPDAUGHTER What do you mean? If the author himself wanted me to be like that! *(She moves over to the DIRECTOR as if to speak to him in confidence.)* I think, sir, that it was rather because of his discouragement or his contempt for the theater as the public generally understands it or wants it to be....

DIRECTOR Let's proceed! Let's proceed, for God's sake, and let's get to the action, my friends!

STEPDAUGHTER Ah, well, excuse me, but it seems to me we have more than enough action with our arrival at his house! *(indicating the FATHER)* You said you couldn't put up signs or change scenery every five minutes!

DIRECTOR Right! Exactly! You have to combine the events, group them in a simultaneous and compact action, and not — as you would have it — first show your little brother coming home from school and wandering like a ghost through the rooms of the house, hiding behind doors to contemplate an idea — how did you put it?

STEPDAUGHTER He's sucking himself dry, sir. He's sucking himself completely dry!

DIRECTOR I've never heard such an expression! You mean, "only his eyes are growing," right?

STEPDAUGHTER Yes, sir. There he is! *(She points to him, close to their MOTHER.)*

DIRECTOR Very good! And now, at the same time, you'd like the little girl too, playing, unaware, in the garden. One in the house, the other in the garden. Is that possible?

STEPDAUGHTER Yes, in the sun, sir. And happy! That's my only reward: her joy, playing in that garden away from poverty, from the squalor of that horrible room where we all four slept — and me with her, imagine! With the horror of my contaminated body next to her, hugging me tight, tight with her loving and innocent little arms. In the garden, as soon as she saw me, she ran to take me by the hand. She didn't want the big flowers. She went looking for the tiny ones and came to show them to me. Making a party of it! A celebration! *(Having said this, tormented by the memory, she breaks out in a long and desperate cry, her head on her arms, which are stretched out on the table. Everyone is overcome with compassion. The DIRECTOR goes up to her, almost paternally.)*

DIRECTOR *(to comfort her)* We'll do the garden. We'll do the garden. Don't worry. And you'll see that you'll be happy with it! We'll group the scenes over there. *(calling by name one of the STAGEHANDS)* Hey there, bring me down some tree branches! Two little cypresses there in front of this pool! *(Two little cypress trees fall from above the stage. The HEAD STAGEHAND runs up to nail down the two bases.)*

DIRECTOR *(to the STEPDAUGHTER)* Just thrown together for now to give an idea. *(calls the STAGEHAND by name again)* Hey there, give me a little sky!

STAGEHAND *(from above)* What?

DIRECTOR A little sky! A backdrop to fall here behind this pool! *(A white cloth falls down from above the stage.)* Not white! I told you sky! Oh well, never mind. I'll take care of it. *(calling out)* Hey, electrician, shut off all the lights, and give me some atmosphere — lunar atmosphere — blue, blue on the striplights and blue on the backdrop, with the reflector.... That's it! *(A mysterious moonlit scene has been created on command, one that will induce the ACTORS to speak and move as if they were in a garden in the evening, under the moon.)*

DIRECTOR *(to the STEPDAUGHTER)* Here it is. Look! Now instead of hiding behind doors in the house, the boy could prowl around here in the garden, hiding behind the trees. But you have to understand that it's going to be hard to find a little girl capable of acting the scene with you when she shows you the tiny flowers. *(addressing the YOUNG BOY)* You, come over here! Let's try to arrange things a bit. *(when the YOUNG BOY doesn't move)* Come on! Come on! *(then pulling him forward, trying to make him hold his head up when it falls down every time)* Ah, another problem.

This boy.... What's the matter with him? For heaven's sake, he's going to have to say something.... *(He goes up to him, puts a hand on his shoulder and leads him behind the trees.)* Come here. Come over here. Let me see! Try to hide here... that's it.... Try to stick your head out a little, to spy.... *(He moves back to see the effect. The YOUNG BOY carries out the action to the consternation of the ACTORS, who are deeply affected by it.)* Oh, excellent, excellent.... *(addressing the STEPDAUGHTER)* And now, what if the little girl, catching him spying like that, runs up to him and drags a couple of words out of his mouth?

STEPDAUGHTER *(rising to her feet)* There's no chance that he'll speak as long as *that one* is here! *(indicating the SON)* You'd have to send him away first.

SON *(moving decisively toward one of the staircases)* I'm ready! More than happy! I couldn't ask for anything better!

DIRECTOR *(quickly, holding him back)* No! Where are you going? Wait! *(The MOTHER rises, worried, anguished by the thought that he is really leaving. She instinctively raises her arms as if to hold him back, but without moving from her place.)*

SON *(at the front of the stage, to the DIRECTOR who is holding him back)* I have nothing to do here, nothing! Let me go, I beg you! Let me leave!

DIRECTOR What do you mean you have nothing to do here?

STEPDAUGHTER *(calmly, ironically)* Don't bother holding him back! He won't leave!

FATHER He has to play the horrifying scene in the garden with his mother.

SON *(quickly, decisively, proudly)* I won't play anything! And I've told you so from the beginning! *(to the DIRECTOR)* Let me go!

STEPDAUGHTER *(running up to the DIRECTOR)* With your permission, sir? *(She has him lower his arms which are holding back the SON.)* Let go of him! *(addressing the SON, as soon as the DIRECTOR lets go of him)* Go ahead, leave!

The SON remains headed for the stairs, but as if bound by a supernatural power, he cannot go down. Then, to the amazement and distress of the ACTORS, he moves slowly along the front of the stage toward the other staircase. Once he reaches it, however, he remains there, unable to go down. The STEPDAUGHTER, *who has been watching him defiantly, bursts out laughing.*

STEPDAUGHTER He can't, you see. He can't! He's bound to stay here; bound by an unbreakable chain. I take off when what must happen comes to pass, precisely because of the hatred I feel for him, because I can't stand his presence. Well if *I* am still here, putting up with him, how do you think he could leave? He is bound to stay here with his fine father and his mother there, who together have no other children besides him. *(addressing the* MOTHER*)* Come on, mamma, come here.... *(addressing the* DIRECTOR, *pointing at the* MOTHER*)* Look, she got up. She got up to hold him back.... *(to the* MOTHER, *as if attracting her by a magical power)* Come, come.... *(then to the* DIRECTOR*)* Imagine what courage it takes for her to show your actors here what she is feeling. But her yearning to be near him is so great that — there, you see? — she's ready to live her scene! *(In fact, the* MOTHER *has drawn near to the* SON, *and as soon as the* STEPDAUGHTER *has pronounced her last words, she opens her arms to signify that she consents.)*

SON *(breaking in)* Oh, but I'm not! I'm not! If I can't leave, I'll stay here, but I'm telling you again that I'm not going to play anything!

FATHER *(trembling with rage, to the* DIRECTOR*)* You can force him, sir.

SON No one can force me!

FATHER *I* will force you!

STEPDAUGHTER Wait! Wait! First, the little girl at the pool. *(She runs to get the* LITTLE GIRL, *falls on her knees before her and holds her little face between her hands.)* My poor little angel, you're looking around bewildered with those big beautiful eyes. Who knows where you think you are? We're on a stage, my dear! What is a stage? Well, you see? It's a place where you play at being serious. You act out plays here. And we'll play-act too. But seriously, you know! Even you.... *(She hugs the* LITTLE GIRL, *holding her tightly to her breast, rocking her a little.)* Oh my sweet love, my little angel, what a horrible play you will act in. What a terrible thing has been thought up for you! The garden, the pool.... It's make-believe, you know! And that's the trouble, my pretty one. Everything is make-believe here! But maybe, my child, you'd rather play in a pretend pool than in a real one. Well, no, it will be a game for the others; not for you, alas, because you're real, my angel, and you are really playing in a real pool, beautiful, big and green. There are lots of bamboos giving it shade, reflected in it, and lots of little ducklings swimming on it, breaking up the shade. You want to catch one, one of those ducklings.... *(with a cry that fills everyone with terror)* No, my Rosetta, no! Mamma's not watching over you because of that beastly son there! My head is full of devils.... And that boy there.... *(She leaves the LITTLE GIRL and addresses the YOUNG BOY with her usual expression.)* What are you doing still here, looking like a beggar? It's your fault too, because of the way you act, if that little one drowns. As if I hadn't paid for all of you, giving you a home! *(grabbing him by the arm to make him take his hand out of his pocket)* What do you have there? What are you hiding? Out, out with that hand! *(She pulls his hand out of his pocket and, to everyone's horror, reveals that he is gripping a revolver. She looks at him a while as if satisfied, and then says in a low voice)* Ah, where, how, did you get it? *(and since the YOUNG BOY, stunned, his eyes still wide-open and empty, does not respond)* You fool. If I were you, instead of killing myself, I would have killed one of those two, or both of them: father and son! *(She pushes him back behind the cypress, where he had been spying. Then she takes the LITTLE GIRL and lowers her into the pool, laying her down so that she remains hidden. Finally, she collapses there herself, her face between her hands, which are resting on the edge of the pool.)*

DIRECTOR Excellent! *(addressing the SON)* And at the same time...

SON *(with contempt)* What do you mean, "at the same time"? It's not true, sir! There *was* no scene between me and her! *(indicating the MOTHER)* Make her tell you herself, how it went.

In the meantime the SUPPORTING ACTRESS and the YOUNG ACTOR have distanced themselves from the group of ACTORS, the former very attentively observing the MOTHER, who stands in front of her, and the latter, the SON, so that they can play their roles.)

MOTHER Yes, it's true, sir. I went into his room.

SON Into my room! You hear? Not in the garden!

DIRECTOR But that doesn't matter! We have to regroup the action, as I said!

SON *(noticing the YOUNG ACTOR observing him)* What do *you* want?

YOUNG ACTOR Nothing. I'm observing you.

SON *(turning to the other side, to the SUPPORTING ACTRESS)* Oh, and there *you* are. To play her role? *(indicating the MOTHER)*

DIRECTOR Exactly! Exactly! And it seems to me that you should be grateful for their attention!

SON Oh sure. Thanks! But don't you understand yet that you can't make this play? We are not in the slightest inside of you, and your actors are there watching us from the outside. Does it seem to you possible to live in front of a mirror that not only freezes the image of our expression and furthermore, throws it back at us as an unrecognizable grimace?

FATHER It's true! It's true! Believe us!

DIRECTOR *(to the YOUNG ACTOR and the SUPPORTING ACTRESS)* Ok, get away from them.

SON It's useless. I'm not having anything to do with this.

DIRECTOR Please be quiet for now, and let me listen to your mother! *(to the MOTHER)* Well then, you went in?

MOTHER Yes, sir, into his room, since I couldn't stand it anymore. To clear my heart of all the anguish oppressing me. But as soon as he saw me come in....

SON No scene! I went away. I left so as not to make a scene. Because *I* have never made scenes! Do you understand?

MOTHER It's true! That's the way he is! The way he is!

DIRECTOR But now we have to do that scene, between you and him. It's indispensable!

MOTHER It's fine with me, sir! If you could just give me the chance to talk to him for a moment, so that I could tell him all that's in my heart....

FATHER *(approaching the SON, violently)* You'll do it! For your mother! For your mother!

SON *(more resolute than ever)* I'll do nothing!

FATHER *(grabbing him by the lapels and shaking him)* By God, obey! Obey! Don't you hear how she's speaking to you? Don't you have a son's heart?

SON *(grabbing him too)* No! No! And end this once and for all! *(General agitation. The MOTHER, terrified, tries to come between them, to separate them.)*

MOTHER *(as above)* For the love of God. Please!

FATHER *(without letting go of him)* You must obey! You must obey!

SON *(wrestling with him and in the end, to everyone's horror, throwing him to the ground near the staircase)* But what is this frenzy that's taken hold of you? He doesn't have the decency to refrain from revealing his shame and ours to everyone! I'll have nothing to do with this! Nothing! And that's how I interpret the will of the author who didn't want to put us on the stage.

DIRECTOR But you all came here.

SON *(pointing to the FATHER) He* did. *I* didn't!

DIRECTOR Aren't you here too?

SON He's the one who decided to come, dragging us all along and even offering to put together with you over there in that office not only what actually happened — as if that weren't enough — but also what didn't happen!

DIRECTOR Well then, tell me. At least you can tell me what happened! Tell me! You came out of your room, without saying anything?

SON *(after a moment's hesitation)* Nothing. Because I didn't want to make a scene!

DIRECTOR *(urging him on)* Well then, what happened next? What did you do?

SON *(taking a few steps on the front of the stage while everyone watches anxiously)* Nothing...crossing the garden.... *(He interrupts himself, gloomy, lost in thought.)*

DIRECTOR *(urging him on, struck by his reticence)* Well then? Crossing the garden?

SON *(exasperated, hiding his face with his arm)* But why do you want to force me to say it, sir? It's horrible! *(The MOTHER, trembling all over, with stifled moans, gazes toward the pool.)*

DIRECTOR *(softly, observing her gaze, addresses the SON with growing apprehension)* The little girl?

SON *(looking straight ahead toward the audience)* There, in the pool....

FATHER *(still on the ground, indicates the MOTHER, with pity)* And she was following him, sir!

DIRECTOR *(to the SON, with anxiety)* And then, you?

SON *(slowly, still looking straight ahead)* I ran. I rushed to pull her out.... But all of a sudden I stopped, because behind those trees I saw something that made my blood turn cold. The boy! The boy was standing still — his eyes like a madman's — gazing at his little sister drowned in the pool. *(The STEPDAUGHTER, still bent over the pool to hide the LITTLE GIRL, answers in a voice like an echo from the depths, sobbing hopelessly. Pause.)* I started to walk up to him, and then.... *(From behind the trees, where the YOUNG BOY has remained hidden, a gunshot rings out.)*

MOTHER *(with a piercing cry, running with the SON, with all the ACTORS in turmoil)* My son! My son! *(and then, amid the confusion and the incoherent cries of the others)* Help! Help!

DIRECTOR *(amid the cries, trying to push his way through, while the YOUNG BOY is lifted by the head and the feet and taken away behind the white backdrop)* Did he wound himself? Did he really wound himself?

Everyone except the DIRECTOR and the FATHER, who is still on the ground next to the staircase, has gone off behind the lowered backdrop and stays there for a while, muttering anxiously. Then, from both sides of the backdrop, the ACTORS come back on stage.

LEAD ACTRESS *(re-entering from the right, sorrowful)* He's dead! Poor boy! He's dead! How awful!

LEAD ACTOR *(re-entering from the left, laughing)* What do you mean, dead?? It's fiction! Fiction! Don't believe it!

OTHER ACTORS FROM THE RIGHT Fiction? Reality! It's reality! He's dead!

OTHER ACTORS FROM THE LEFT No! Fiction! Fiction!

FATHER *(getting up and shouting among them)* What do you mean, fiction? Reality, ladies and gentlemen, reality! *(He too goes off behind the backdrop, in despair.)*

DIRECTOR *(unable to stand it anymore)* Fiction! Reality! To hell with all of you! Lights! Lights! Lights! *(Suddenly, the entire stage and the auditorium are filled with a brilliant light. The DIRECTOR breathes deeply as if freed from a nightmare, and all the ACTORS look each other in the eyes, bewildered and confused.)* Ah! Nothing like this ever happened to me! They made me waste a whole day! *(He looks at his watch.)* Go on, go on! What more can be done? It's too late to start the rehearsal again. See you tonight! *(And as soon as the ACTORS leave, saying goodbye to him)* Hey, electrician! Turn everything off! *(Even before he finishes saying it, the theater falls in an instant into total darkness.)* For God's sake! Leave at least a little light on, so I can see where to put my feet!

Immediately, behind the backdrop, as if by mistake, a green spotlight goes on, projecting large and distinct shadows of the CHARACTERS, except for the YOUNG BOY and the LITTLE GIRL. When the DIRECTOR sees them, he runs from the stage terrified. At the same time, the spotlight behind the backdrop goes off, and the stage is lit by the blue of the night sky as before. Slowly, from the right side of the curtain, the SON steps forward first, followed by the MOTHER with her arms stretched out toward him, then, from the left side, the FATHER. They stop in the center, remaining there, dreamlike shapes. Last, the STEPDAUGHTER enters from the left. She runs toward one stairway. On the first step she stops a moment to look at the other three and breaks out in a strident laugh. Then she rushes down the stairs, runs down the aisle between the seats, stops to laugh once again, looking at the three onstage, and vanishes from the theater. Again, her laughter is heard again from the lobby. Shortly after, the curtain falls.

Sheet music for "Beware of Chou Chin Chow." Provided courtesy of Special Collections, the University of South Florida Libraries.

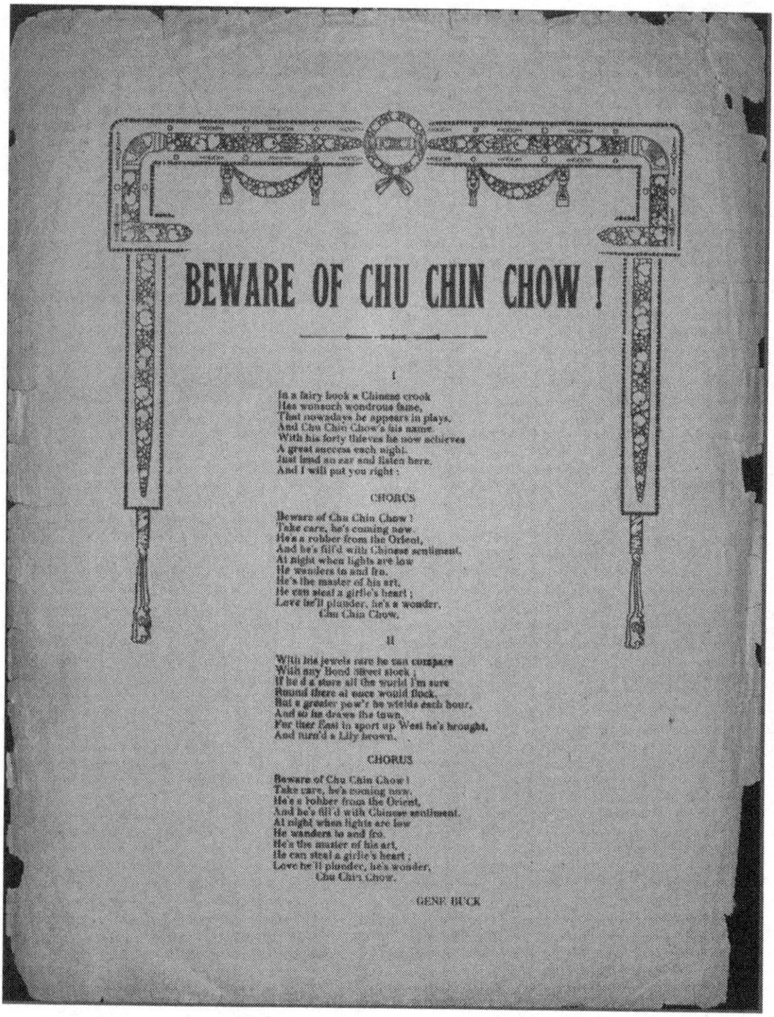

BEWARE OF CHU CHIN CHOW !

I

In a fairy book a Chinese crook
Has wonsuch wondrous fame,
That nowadays he appears in plays,
And Chu Chin Chow's his name.
With his forty thieves he now achieves
A great success each night.
Just lend an ear and listen here,
And I will put you right :

CHORUS

Beware of Chu Chin Chow !
Take care, he's coming now.
He's a robber from the Orient,
And he's fill'd with Chinese sentiment.
At night when lights are low
He wanders to and fro.
He's the master of his art,
He can steal a girlie's heart ;
Love he'll plunder, he's a wonder,
Chu Chin Chow.

II

With his jewels rare he can compare
With any Bond Street stock ;
If he'd a store all the world I'm sure
Round there at once would flock.
But a greater pow'r he wields each hour,
And so he draws the town,
For ther East to sport up West he's brought,
And turn'd a Lily brown.

CHORUS

Beware of Chu Chin Chow !
Take care, he's coming now.
He's a robber from the Orient,
And he's fill'd with Chinese sentiment.
At night when lights are low
He wanders to and fro.
He's the master of his art,
He can steal a girlie's heart ;
Love he'll plunder, he's wonder,
Chu Chin Chow.

GENE BUCK

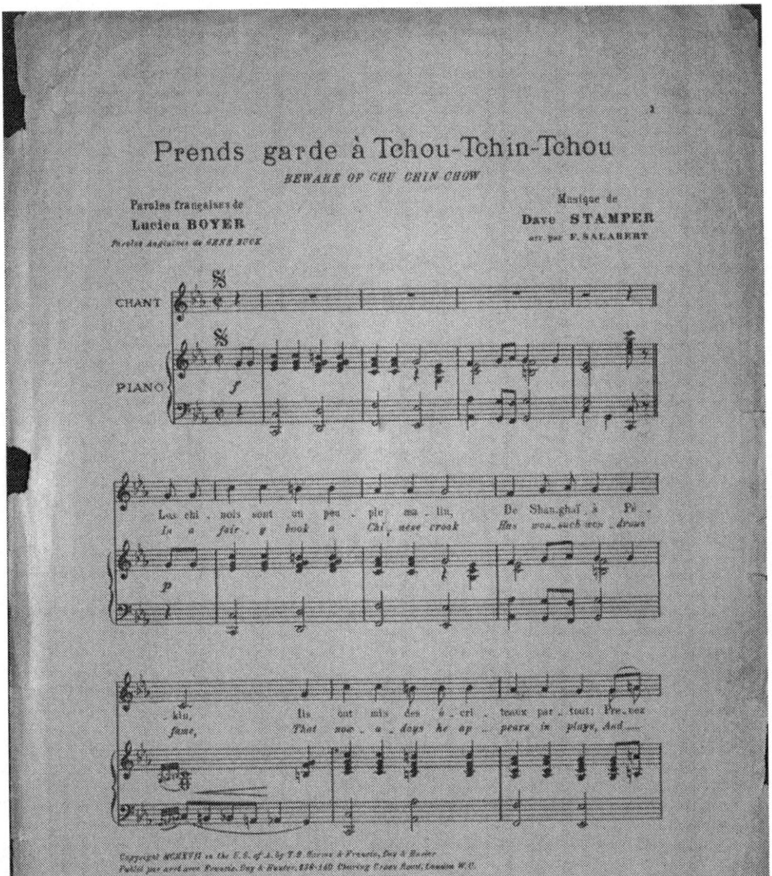
Prends garde à Tchou-Tchin-Tchou
BEWARE OF CHU CHIN CHOW
Paroles françaises de
Lucien BOYER
Musique de
Dave STAMPER
arr. par F. SALABERT
CHANT
PIANO
FRANCIS SALABERT
22, rue Chauchat, Paris

now a-chieves A great suc-cess each night.
lend an ear and lis-ten here, And I will put you right:
REFRAIN
Prends garde à Tchou-Tchin-Tchou!
Be-ware of Chu Chin Chow!

Il vient à pas de
Take care, he's com - ing
loup
now,
Et vous cam - bri - o - le
He's a rob - ber from the
en pas - sant...
O - ri - ent,
And he's
pas vos bi - joux qu'il vous prend!
fill'd with Chi - nese sent - i - ment.
Non,
Ah

ce roi des vo - leurs
night when lights are low
He wan - ders to and fro
Vous con - nais - sez ce fri - pon
He's the mas - ter of his art
Nous l'ap - pe - lons Cu - pi - don
He can steal a girl - ie's heart
Chu Chin Chow!
D.C.

Select Bibliography

Bassnett-McGuire, Susan. *Luigi Pirandello.* New York: Grove Press, 1983.

Bassnett, Susan, and Jennifer Lorch, eds. *Luigi Pirandello in the Theatre: A Documentary Record.* Reading, UK: Harwood Academic, 1993.

Bentley, Eric. *The Pirandello Commentaries.* Evanston, IL: Northwestern University Press, 1986.

Biasin, Gian Paolo, and Manuela Gieri, eds. *Luigi Pirandello: Contemporary Perspectives.* Toronto: University of Toronto Press, 1999.

Bini, Daniela. *Pirandello and His Muse: The Plays for Marta Abba.* Gainesville: University Press of Florida, 1998.

Farrell, Joseph, and Paolo Puppa, eds. *A History of Italian Theatre.* Cambridge: Cambridge University Press, 2006.

DiGaetani, John Louis, ed. *A Companion to Pirandello Studies.* New York: Greenwood Press, 1991.

Giudice, Gaspare. *Pirandello: A Biography.* Translated by A. Hamilton. London: Oxford University Press, 1975.

Lorch, Jennifer. *Pirandello: Six Characters in Search of an Author.* Cambridge: Cambridge University Press, 2005.

Pirandello, Luigi. *On Humor.* Translated by Antonio Illiano and Daniel P. Testa. Chapel Hill: University of North Carolina Press, 1974.

Ragusa, Olga. "Teaching Six Characters." *Italica* 85.1 (Spring 2008): 88–101.

Paolucci, Anne. *Pirandello's Theater: The Recovery of the Modern Stage for Dramatic Art.* Carbondale: Southern Illinois University Press, 1974.

Syska-Lamparska, Rena A., ed. *Ars dramatica: Studi sulla poetica di Luigi Pirandello.* New York: Peter Lang, 1996.

Witt, Mary Ann Frese. *The Search for Modern Tragedy: Aesthetic Fascism in Italy and France.* Ithaca, NY: Cornell University Press, 2001.

—. "*Six Characters in Search of an Author* and the Battle of the Lexis." *Modern Drama* (Sept. 1987): 396–404.

This Book Was Completed on 24 September 2013
at Italica Press, New York. It Is Set in
Adobe Garamond and Prestige
Elite and Printed on
Acid-Free Paper.

74563574R00073

Made in the USA
Columbia, SC
02 August 2017